Washington Lawyers

Based on a true story:
by Nicholas Paleveda MBA J.D. LL.M

1

Published and distributed by Amazon.com
© Nicholas Paleveda 2012
ISBN-13 978-1477576427
ISBN-10 1477576428

Dedicated to the employees who do the
heavy lifting for their companies and the
victims of white collar crime, a 300-600
Billion dollar industry in comparison with
violent crime a 1.19 billion dollar industry.

Chapter1.

WELCOME TO SEATTLE!

I had come to Seattle in 1999 as an attorney from Florida. My wife had family in the Seattle area and knew the area well. My wife's family had founded "Morrison Mills" in Bellingham which at one time was larger than Weyerhaeuser. The Mills were located in Bellingham, Anacortes, Ferndale and Blaine in the early 1900s. The local people were known to be kind and good spirited and people were known to pull together in times of crisis. Reluctantly, but willingly, we went to Seattle driving from Atlanta crossing the great plains in a multiple day drive and establishing residence in the "Emerald City".

Upon arriving in Seattle, I noticed how "green" everything is from the trees and grass. "Why is that?" I asked? "That's because it rains here all the time", she said which is a good answer from an A student. Marjorie had obtained a graduate degree in tax from USC when most women were not obtaining degrees from Business Schools. She graduated with an "A" average at Georgia State. She was the typical student you love to hate, hard working, smart, pulls down good grades. I had a lot of college degrees, and was addicted to Chess winning several State Chess Championships in Florida, but I managed to keep grades at a suboptimal levels. I always appreciated the hard working students who could do so well. In any event we were in Seattle and my business was 2000 miles away. Fortunately there was the internet and flights which kept me in contact with an ever shrinking client base and ever changing tax code.

In January of 2002, I attended the University of Miami Estate Planning Institute. The Institute is one of the oldest and largest gatherings of Estate Planning attorneys in the U.S. Each year in January, nearly 3,000 attorneys make the "Mecca to Miami" to attend the Institute to learn the latest tax law changes for their wealthy clients. The law was changing in the estate tax area. The estate tax was scheduled to be "repealed". During the evenings of the Miami Institute a group of us would get together to discuss legal and tax issues over dinner. John Koresko JD CPA a brilliant tax attorney who was never short for opinions, "412(i), it is a sissy 419 plan" he said. Craig Hampton, J.D. LL.M known as "the professor" due to his encyclopedia knowledge of Estate Planning stated "When it comes to tax planning being a sissy may not be a bad idea". The table was crowded with scholars and lawyers who had many years of tax experience. Frank Murphy J.D. CPA who graduated at the top of his class at Stetson Law School, La Donna Cody J.D. who runs a tax practice in Ft. Myers and

Greg Keane J.D. MBA, CPA, LL.M, LL. M who had more degrees and CE Bar credits then anyone in the State of Florida. Greg also sat on the ethics committee for the Florida Bar. When he was one of our law partners, he would hammer into us the latest ethical rules of the Florida Bar. Recently, George Bush had become President and he vowed to eliminate the "death tax" which effectively would put most estate tax attorneys out of business. "Who needs an estate tax attorney if there is no "estate tax", I asked. "Well, there will always be probate" said Frank Murphy. Frank had helped me pass the bar and was also a master chess player and bridge player. When I came back to Florida, Frank grilled me endlessly with Florida questions so I could pass the crazy exam. Frank, of course, was the first person done with the exam out of the 1,000 persons in the room. Frank Murphy also worked with me at our start-up law firm Hampton, Paleveda, Murphy, Cody and

Levy in the 80s. "What are the options?" I asked "The tax code always provides opportunity" Frank said. The new code EGTRRA 2001 provided the answer. The code was bringing back the old defined benefit pension plan. The problem is I was not an "ERISA" or pension attorney, but this is where the opportunity seems to be heading. Full speed ahead anyway and ... it was time to start a company! I head back to Seattle to start a pension company based on 412(i)!

The Law Firm of Price and Farrington, an estate planning firm sits in the middle of Bel-Red road in Bellevue Washington in a class B building. The 'eclectic' entrance to his office has a cigar smoking Indian; a 7 ft. model of the space needle and is adorned with oriental rugs and meerschaum pipes. It is perhaps one of the most over-decorated offices in America. Glenn Price had started the firm after leaving Morgan Lewis and Brokius, a large Philadelphia law firm, to start his own practice. Glenn had no real business background, but locating 3 miles from Microsoft certainly helped his estate planning practice. Glenn realized he needed a tax expert and hired Charles Farrington who recently completed his LL.M or Masters in Taxation at the University of Miami. I quickly became friends with Glenn and Chuck Farrington on my arrival in Seattle as I knew them from the estate planning attorneys I was in contact with through the internet.

On June 15, 2002 I worked with Charles Farrington to create a Company "PFP plan administrators" bringing along Glenn Price and Charles Farrington and Bill Faiferlick, an insurance agent, as shareholders. Chuck Farrington filled out the legal paperwork, articles of incorporation etc. Bill Faiferlick was to hold the insurance licenses for the company and I would be the moving force behind building the company. The internet world was expanding and it appeared that there was an opportunity to administer pension plans through the internet. Many dotcoms had started in Seattle and many went bust. In 2000, commercial real estate was next to impossible to find, but by 2001, the market had some slack as the boom was turning into a bust. Marjorie, my wife, created the business plan to administer pension plans through the internet. Marjorie also provided the credit to start the company placing the office furniture and equipment on her credit cards. Marjorie had worked with start-ups in the past including home-tax, a precursor to turbo-tax, and several of my fanciful ideas. She also had worked at Price Waterhouse, a large CPA firm, after receiving her Masters in Tax at USC. Glenn Price and Charles Farrington were going to support the legal needs and provide office space.

Unfortunately, stock was issued in the following amount 37.5% to Nick Paleveda,

37.5% to Bill Faiferlick and 25% to Price and Farrington. I wanted to be fair to the participants which later I found not to be a good idea or in English- This was a mistake. I discovered later on- mistake number one-be careful on trusting your attorney friend. I had trusted Glenn and Chuck who were two attorneys he had worked with in the past to work with me on this project, not understanding their true motives. In addition, 50% of the stock was held as Treasury stock. I was elected President and CEO of the 412(i) Company frankly because none of the others had any idea how this would work. The company PFP Plan Administrator a/k/a The 412(i) Company was formed!

Forming a company is the easy part, making the company profitable is the hard part. I put on several seminars in the local area to notify the financial community about the new changes under EGTRRA and the opportunities in pension plans. Time passed with.... no revenue- March,

April, May, June, July, and August.....no revenue. It appeared the project was a failure....a bust! Then, in September of 2002, PFP had its first client, then second, third, etc. It was exciting! Money started to come in and finally Bill Faiferlick and I could get paid! (Glenn and Chuck were not working for the company as employees). A $74,000 check that came into the company to now pay salaries-and when money comes in- this is where the problem started. Marjorie was upset that payroll taxes and income taxes were not taken out-a problem that happened years ago to me in another company, Mutual Benefit Life. The 412(i)company had hired Dawn Brazel, a friend of Glenn Price to be the bookkeeper-and working with Bill Faiferlick and our motley crew, the finances were not being handled properly...a/k/a taxes were not being paid. Marjorie had to start coming into the office to assist and I needed help to make sure the taxes etc get paid.

We really needed the help. The 412(i) Company hired John Ells a high school student who was a computer wiz to develop the website. John had run several school websites and was grateful for the job. The company also needed an experience actuary. I tried to do the calculations and formulas ourselves using a top math student from Shoreline, Hiroshi Kuga, who won math competitions and scored a perfect 800 on his SATs in math. "The math is easy", said Hiroshi, "but the law is difficult". This was a real problem, over 4,000 pages of tax law to review.

The next check that came in and Marjorie made sure the check was used to pay payroll taxes and clean up the accounts, much to the dismay of Glenn and Chuck-who wanted money and Bill Faiferlick. They needed to get rid of Marjorie. Tensions mounted between Bill, Glenn, Chuck and on Labor-day weekend, they walked into the PFP office and announced Marjorie was fired. How sweet. I signed on the lease, Marjorie used her credit cards to buy the computers etc., I had negotiated the insurance contracts and all the contacts from the company were mine and Glenn and Chuck and Bill decided to fire Marjorie because she insisted payroll taxes had to be paid. Chuck Farrington is a Washington tax attorney-he should know better. There were other items they did not like about Marjorie as she disturbed the old boys on Club Bel-Red road, which they outlined in a 100 page paper we received later on.

What to do now?

Chapter 2

CALL IN THE ARMY-I MEAN LAWYER!

Paul Hess J.D. was a local businessman with a law degree from the University of Kansas. He had practiced law in Kansas for many years and served in the State Legislature, the Senate and House. Paul was in his 50s with a white beard and dressed, looked and acted the part of an attorney. Paul had been chief operation officer for many companies in Seattle, including Seminar Masters, EDVITA, Q-Pharma, etc. Paul and his wife, Jan Hess, had told me about Paul's many successful turn-arounds as he was an expert in getting companies off the ground and raising funds for start-ups. "Oh Paul is great at turning companies around" said Jan Hess. "He is also an attorney, just like your husband Nick", she told Marjorie.

I had met Jan and Paul at chess tournaments ran in Kellogg Middle school.

They had volunteered to help out with concessions as their sons John and Matt Ness played on the chess team. I was coaching both of them and they were both intelligent hard working students.

Paul seemed like the correct candidate for the job of removing and replacing Bill Faiferlick. Paul's credentials were impeccable. Attorney in Kansas, served on the Kansas legislature, expert at turning around companies, experience lawyer and negotiator, just what the situation called for to bring the company together.

I met with Marjorie and Paul at Elena's, a diner in Shoreline. Paul explained his background as a COO, Chief Operations Officer for many of the start-up companies in Seattle and how he and Jan were turning around Q-Pharma. Once he was done with that job he would be available to help with ours. We hired him to represent us, and he said he knew exactly what to do.

I arraigned a meeting with Paul and Glenn at the Law offices of Price and Farrington. Glenn was impressed with Paul and his credentials, serving in politics and lawyer and COO for many local companies. Glenn had always wanted to be successful in politics but unfortunately lost a college election to Al Gore, yes "the Al Gore" while Glenn attended Harvard. Al Gore went on to become Vice President and Glenn became an estate planning attorney in Bellevue.

Paul was convincing as he plead our case, which was quite simple at the time. The idea was Nick's, all the contacts were his, all the contracts he negotiated, Nick had the lease and Marjorie bought all the equipment. Frankly all PFP had was stock. Paul liked private meetings, so he met privately with Glenn and Chuck then finally with Bill Faiferlick in a private room. Paul was overheard yelling and screaming at Bill Faiferlick. In spite of the turmoil, we wanted to be fair to Bill and give him stock or something, but it appeared to be a shouting match and Bill left, never to come back. What was said, what was done, only Bill and Paul know for sure. After the meeting Paul said, "That was easy, I thought he would put up a better fight then that." Paul relished in the victory over Bill.

The tensions in the company had come to an end, or at least we thought they did.

In November of 2002 the 412(i) Company was reorganized giving Nick 82.5% of the stock, Price and Farrington Law Firm 12.5% of the stock and Paul 2.5% of the stock. Paul had provided the company with the removal of Bill Faiferlick to solve a dispute between Bill and Marjorie. Charles Farrington now held the corporate insurance license as he was an insurance agent as well as an attorney. Hess was invited to join the company as a part time consultant in November of 2003. Glenn Price was so impressed that after the meeting with Bill Faiferlick he invited

Paul to become "of counsel" to his firm Price and Farrington. Paul said he would have to "think about it". Opportunities were opening up for Paul as "of counsel" attorney to the Law Firm of Price and Farrington or COO of the 412(i) Company. Paul turned down the "of counsel" attorney position. "I have been the COO for many other companies and as an attorney would be available for full time COO position at the 412(i)Company starting in January of 2003" he said.

Time passed and in February of 2003 I met with Paul to review the COO of the company and a full time employee. "What are your salary requirements? I asked." Paul said $80,000.00. We then agreed to give him a salary of $85,000 per year. once again, I wanted to be more than fair with Paul and I insisted on the increase. The 412(i)company was also looking to move away from Bellevue/Redmond as Microsoft really dominated the area. We looked around the area, Tacoma, Yakima,

Spokane, Mt. Vernon and Bellingham. Seattle's traffic could only get worse and the real estate market was already becoming expensive as we were so close to Microsoft's world headquarters.

Chapter 3

What is Bellingham?

What is Bellingham? The "City of subdued excitement!" Off the map and to the north of Seattle lies a community that time stood still or Bellingham Washington. An annual protest (for 30 years) takes place at the Federal Building every Friday afternoon. Hippies with grey pony tails (like Ivan) line the downtown area, and franchise stores are basically not allowed. The dress code is predominantly "goodwill" clothes on special and the farmers market delights the town each Saturday during the summer. Steve Moore was the commercial realtor in Bellingham, and like most of Bellingham, the only commercial Realtor. Bellingham had one Wal-Mart, One Costco, one Holiday Inn, one Best Buy and frankly one of everything but not two. These stores, perhaps because they were "chain" stores were "forbidden" inside the

Interstate beltway. Inside the "beltway" chains meant growth and "growth" is bad. South of downtown is Western Washington University which was established in the late 1800's as the teachers college in Washington. South of "Western" as the locals call it, is Fairhaven a tourist trap or Yuppie community, and home to the "Alaska Ferry", a ferry that can take you to Alaska sponsored by the State.

Bellingham had not much to do with Seattle, and frankly not much to do with the USA. You have to drive through a mountain pass to get there and it is surrounded by mountains to the south and east and Bellingham Bay to the west. The only way out is Canada to the north. Now Steve Moore had grown up in Orange County but fell in love with Bellingham and would not go back. The Bellingham Chamber of Commerce brought together Steve, Kent Balma a banker from Key Bank and others to welcome us to

Bellingham. We were escorted by Steve around Bellingham to look at commercial properties. Everything was less then Redmond, Seattle or Bellevue. What a nice place to start an internet company. We settled on The Pacific Meridian Building, a nice class "A" office space outside the "beltway".

The move to Bellingham was not supported by everyone. Paul and Erik, one of our employees, wanted to stay in Bellevue, so we made accommodations for them. Charles Gramp-our newly hired chief actuary, who moved from North Carolina to become the Chief Actuary, could not make the switch until the following year. We kept an office in Bellevue to accommodate some of the employees, while the others went to Bellingham. During this time I was negotiating contracts with Hartford, Pacific Life, Mass Mutual to handle their plan administration. On one trip I went with Paul to Boston to meet with senior officers of Mass Mutual, Tom Monte and Josh Hazelwood. I had also attempted to line up attorney Mary Young from Hartford and home office persons from Lincoln National. The trip was long from Seattle to Boston and return and I had plenty of time to talk to Paul about the company and business objectives etc. Paul wanted to share his "bonus" structure for the company. I thought it would be a good idea, if the company was sound. Paul talked about a bonus plan for himself and gave me a document which I reviewed but could not agree on as the company was only operational for 6 months and tying the company into bonuses would not be favorable at this time. Paul said that was fine, if the company did not do well then the bonuses would not be paid of course. I thought it was odd that he would say this and give me an agreement, but in any event I did not sign it but would review it later on.

Paul had suggested the company needed to give the employees an incentive to continue working at the company. Paul suggested .05% for Sharon Angel, .05% for Doug Farrar, 2.5% for Eirk Shaner and 8% for Paul. Paul explained the bonuses would be non-binding. Paul agreed the bonus structure needed to be non-binding as the company was a start-up company. Paul assured me that would be the case. Paul presented a written contract for himself at 8%. This also presented a problem. Why is his amount so much larger than the other employees? I informed Paul he would need an insurance license to receive bonuses. Paul said he would get an insurance license and it would not be a problem.

Chapter 4

MONEY!

The company was growing fast. Each day I
was on the phone with producers and
insurance companies. Mass Mutual,
Transamerica, American General,
Hartford. This kept me occupied on a full
time basis. I was creating the operations of
the company and Charles Gramp was
putting together the plan designs.
Everyone was busy- real busy. We had
hired John Bremer and enrolled actuary
and CPA from PriceWaterhouseCoopers in
Chicago to take over the administration
and review Charles Gramp's work.
It was good to know that a team was
forming. Price and Farrington, the law
firm, would work out the legal aspects of
the company. Charles Farrington would
hold the Insurance licenses and Paul Hess
would operate as chief operations officer

and General Counsel, a position he brought years of experience to the table. Every day Paul Hess came into the office he spent hours with Sharon Angel, the bookkeeper reviewing the books and records of the company. Paul as attorney and COO had access to the entire organization. "I have experience getting companies off the ground". Paul said. The company was in start-up mode. The files were disorganized and the systems had not been in place yet to smoothly run the operation. Charles Gramp seemed to know everything about pensions, but Paul was the "salesman". Paul could talk to the clients and producers and had the legal credentials needed to keep the company out of trouble, Paul was a trusted attorney from Kansas and spent years in the Kansas legislature. "We don't want to get involved in abusive tax schemes" he said to one producer. "We have professional licenses at stake". This was reassuring as ethics and integrity are important to any professional organization. Florida was strict in disciplining attorneys who did the slightest unethical behavior. Soliciting business, advertising without bar approval, not responding to clients, all subject attorneys to bar disciplinary action. I felt comfortable that I had another attorney Paul Hess watching over the organization.

In July of 2003, Paul realized that a check in the amount of $146,181.90 was coming to the company. Paul had spent an enormous time with the bookkeeper Sharon Angel who could not understand why he was preoccupied about the revenues of the company. Paul had also visited each employee separately behind closed doors to gain insight about each individual to make sure they were doing their jobs. Many of the employees respected Paul who had years of business and legal experience. We decided that our additional operation in Bellevue would be too expensive for a growing company and decided to close Bellevue. Microsoft about 3 miles from our headquarters started buying real estate in the area. Several years back, Glenn Price and I had traveled to Bellingham about 90 miles north of Seattle which had beauty and more important, low rent and labor cost. From August 2002 until March of 2003, I made trips to Yakima, Tacoma, Lynwood, Mt. Vernon, Blaine and the surrounding area near Seattle. In most cases rents were high except Bellingham. I recalled my days in Florida that most really wealthy people "opted out" of the large cities like Miami and Tampa for the smaller towns of Boca Raton and Naples. It seemed clear to me that Bellingham was that small town, a college town with Western Washington University at its doorstep and a large medical facility, St. Joseph's Hospital. Bellingham was indeed not Boca. The people were laid back in Bellingham, so laid back the city looked as if it never left the 60s. I guess that was the charm of the city, grey haired hippies, professors, physicians and a small business community. Unlike Blaine, another beautiful city to the north, we were happy we decided to move the main office from Bellevue to Bellingham where the rent and cost of business was lower, but now we were moving the rest of the operation to Bellingham. We proceeded to rent additional space in Bellingham according to plan however, Paul Hess had another plan for the company.

Chapter 5

EMBEZZLEMENT!

"Criminals with law degrees"

August 8, is to be remembered as the day Richard Nixon resigned. This day it falls between the day the bomb was dropped on Hiroshima on August 6th and Nagasaki August 9th, and the day Hess e-mailed me a note that the check of $146,181.90 that we were looking for and had gone missing for two weeks was taken by Hess, Price, and Farrington. There would be no money for payroll or rent as this was money to be used for their "bonuses"!

If you want to steal money from an individual or corporation, accuse them of stealing money! Paul Hess was a master at this concept. The official letter written by Hess and signed by Glenn Price and Charles Farrington stated as follows:

Dear Nick and Marjorie:

"This letter is written following your refusal to accept Paul Hess' request of August 2 and August 4, 2003 to meet with you immediately to discuss the serious corporate matters which are now addressed herein.

We currently hold the following corporate positions in PFP:

Hess: Chief Operating Officer of PFP

Price: Director and Vice President of PFP

Farrington: Director and Secretary/Treasurer of PFP

After numerous lengthy discussions in recent weeks and consultation with two attorneys and a CPA, the three of us unanimously conclude that we no longer can, in good faith, continue to be associated in any corporate or formal capacity with PFP as directors, officers, employees, consultants/licensed agent or any other capacity, except to fulfill our fiduciary responsibility in those roles. This decision is based upon the following factors we have experienced in your operation of the company.

- Gross mismanagement of corporate affairs;
- Misappropriation of corporate funds for personal use;
- Arrogation of title and authority without formal approval or accountability;
- Failure to satisfy company commitments regarding compensation ;
- Failure to consider state law regarding licensure issues.
- Failure to obtain Directors and Officers Insurance

The activities described in this letter are attributed to Nick Paleveda President and CEO ("Paleveda") and Marjorie Ewing("Ewing"), who is Paleveda's wife. Marjorie Ewing does not have and never had an official, Board of Directors ("Board")-authorized appointment or position with PFP as an officer, director or in any other executive position. Except for her personal relationship with Nick Paleveda as his spouse, Marjorie Ewing's increasing and now near –total control of PFP's affairs has no legitimate basis or authorization. Ewing has acted in the self-appointed capacity of "Senior Executive Vice President" with no authority from, or accountability to, the Board. In August 2002, by unanimous resolution of the Board, Ewing was summarily ad permanently dismissed from any and all involvement, activity and association with PFP.

The resolution was signed by Paul Glenn and Chuck-but not me! Wait a minute I am on the board!

This was an interesting letter, obviously full of hate by Glenn Chuck and Paul. What followed was obvious.

"What follows constitutes the reasons for the actions we have taken in this letter in our fiduciary roles as officers and directors."

Our Fiduciary obligation to take all the money out of the corporation and give it to ourselves! This is a new one. Can you imagine a bank robber explaining that he is holding up the bank because he has a fiduciary obligation to take the funds? We also take all the money to ourselves in "good faith". Only a lawyer could think of this, or a criminal with a law degree.

And the actions were quite simple, the lawyers took all the money out of the company and paid bonuses to themselves with tiny other amounts going to employees leaving the company...well.....broke. I never understood that a fiduciary has an obligation to take all the money out of a company and give themselves bonuses. This must be a new law in Washington. In this case, the amount was about $146,181.90 and the company was broke. Here is Glenn Price and Chuck Farrington the "Washington Lawyer" interpretation.

"Washington state law provides that compensation to employees includes salaries, wages, bonuses, commissions and severance pay in lieu of salary or wages. The bonuses delineated above were agreed to by Paleveda and Ewing and committed to be paid in full by you on or before July 31, 2003 on all 2002 cases and renewals based on gross commissions earned or to be earned by PFP.

The officers and directors of a corporation in Washington State are personally liable for all compensation, as defined above, promised to employees that have not been paid by the corporation. Interest at the statutory judgment rate of 8% annually is also allowed the employee against officers and directors personally for unpaid compensation. Officers and directors are also personally liable under federal statute for all required federal income tax, FICA and Medicare withholding not submitted and paid by the corporation to the government for each employee, including substantial penalties and interest if paid late.

Based on the above, as officers and directors of PFP, we could have, jointly and severally, substantial personal liability for decisions taken by Paleveda and Ewing regarding compensation and potential failure to pay required government withholdings. This personal liability stems from Paleveda's and Ewing's actions, including hiring and budgeting decisions, control of the corporate checkbooks, and failure to pay promised compensation to certain employees. We also would be liable in the event of Paleveda's and Ewing's failure to meet a payroll in the near term as a result of mismanagement and diversion of corporate funds. Under these circumstances, we no longer can or will continue to hold positions in the company as officers and directors which could result in substantial personal liability."

Signed

Glenn, Chuck and Paul

Bottom line is now that we were DEMONIZED we will take all the money out of the company and put it in our own pockets. –So there! Price and Farrington cried and complain about their "liability "so they can embezzle the money and leave the company broke. A brilliant play, but who masterminded this play? Was it Price, Farrington or Hess?

These three attorneys were now operating as one unit to grab as much money on the table and leave the employees without possibility of being paid as the company bank was broke.

It was a shock to receive such a notice. The timing was also brilliant. During those two weeks our staff was putting on an educational seminar for attorneys and CPAs around the U.S. relating to defined benefit plans. Why everyone was working to move the company forward, the thieves were working to steal the money out of the company.

The following day I went to the Bellevue Police. The story was laid out to the police on Monday morning and the police did their homework. I sat at the police station and waited. Finally one of the officers comes out- "Well you have a live one here", he said. "What do you mean?" I said. That Paul Hess, he's not an attorney, he is a convicted felon. Convictions for theft, securities fraud, and forgery trafficking in illegal goods......I was in shock, not only did we have $146,181.90 embezzled before our eyes; Paul Hess, the attorney who was our general counsel was not an attorney at all but..... A convicted felon!

Chapter 6

PAUL HESS J.D.

Paul Hess J.D. was charged on November 16, 1985 with two counts of felony theft. These charges grew out of allegations that Mr. Hess had misappropriated funds belonging to clients and received by Mr. Hess. According to court records the charges grew out of allegations that Mr. Hess had misappropriated funds belonging to clients and received by Mr. Hess in the course of representing these clients. On the 7th day of January 1985, Mr. Hess entered into a plea agreement and pled guilty to one count of felony theft. The other count was dismissed. Mr. Hess had disciplinary proceedings against him in Kansas and surrendered his license to practice law and entered prison. But Paul did not enter prison voluntarily. Once his victims in Kansas got wind of his theft and the police

started to track him down, Paul left
Kansas with his children and fled to Cairo
Egypt. Anne Oliver Hess, his spouse and
police officer Hank Goodman tracked
down Hess and the boys in Cairo Egypt. At
a Parole Board public comment session in
June, Goodman opposed parole for Hess.
He said Hess had threatened him at the
American Embassy in Cairo. He told me
"he'd get me if it took him the rest of his
life." Goodman said. Hess began serving
time in July 1986 in the maximum
security section of the Kansas State
Penitentiary at Lansing. His sentence from
Linn County was one to three years. Hess,
prior to his convictions, was elected to the
Legislature from a Wichita district and
was chairman of its Ways and Means
committee; one of the most influential
positions in the Senate. The parole board
stated, "The board including me, felt that
he was very forthright (in interviews with
the board), that he had done a
considerable amount of introspection and

had really examined himself and saw where he did make his errors" said Elaine Pomeroy. No truer words were spoken. Paul was able to see his error-he got caught. However, the board released him. "He's a very intelligent man," Hetzel said, "I think his main objective was to work himself through the system and obtain parole as soon as possible and get on with his life". Hess had forged the names of his wife and mother in law on loan papers, for this he was sentenced to 5 years in prison. Hess had also embezzled $14,500 from an insurance settlement that was meant for two of his clients. For this he was sentenced to 3 years probation. "He suffered a lot" Elaine Pomercy, chairman of the parole board and friend of Paul Hess stated. Mr. Pomeroy had served with Hess in the Kansas senate. Hess had also pleaded guilty to two counts of securities fraud for issuing bogus stock certificates to two persons. He was sentenced to one year in prison on each charge to run concurrently with his forgery sentence, and ordered to make restitution. Hess was also sued by a Kansas City woman Velma Todd for embezzling $38,545.00 of a trust Todd's attorney Allen Libovitz said the trust agreements were produced but their authenticity was questionable. Oliver's signature may have been forged, the suit contends.

After Paul was released in Kansas, he was arrested again in Washington. In 1990, Mary Summers, the Deputy Prosecuting Attorney in Whatcom County where Bellingham is located accused and indicted Paul Hess for possession and transport of untaxed cigarettes in excess of $60,000. In Washington, this was a felony indictment. According to the affidavit for probable cause On November 24, 1992 and December 2, 1992 at 79 Tyree Road, Point Roberts, Whatcom County Washington, Paul Hess and Willem Alphenaar, manager of the Washington State Liquor Store #641 knowingly or intentionally possessed or transported more than $60,000 contraband untaxed cigarettes. On November 23, 1992 U.S. Custom Agents and members of the Canadian RCMP were advised of a possible delivery of contraband unstamped cigarettes to Point Roberts Washington. Point Roberts Auto Freight became concerned that the circulars they were to deliver contained pornographic material. When they opened the cases for examination, rather than pornographic material, they discovered unstamped contraband. The freight charges were paid in cash by Mr. Alphenaar. The code name for the cigarettes was "circulars". A controlled delivery was made to the liquor store location. Supervising Revenue Officer Maine Peace Jr. obtained a search warrant for the liquor store premises due to the delivery of the contraband cigarettes to a Washington location. Possession and or transportation of untaxed cigarettes in

Washington to anyone but an authorized wholesale cigarette dealer is a class "C" felony pursuant to Washington law. The delivery was made on November 24 1992 at 10:00 a.m. Officer Peace executed the search warrant with the assistance of the Whatcom Sheriff's department and U.S. Customs and the RCMP. In the back room of the liquor store were located 15 cases delivered on November 24 1992 and an additional 13 cases of contraband cigarettes from an earlier shipment. The search warrant was served on an employee of the store as Mr. Alphenaar was not in the store at the time of the service. Mr. Alphenaar was contacted by his employee and arrived during the inventory of the seized cigarettes. Mr. Alphenaar denied any knowledge of the contents of the cigarettes that was delivered. During a final search of the premises, an additional 3 cases were found commingled with the liquor stores' regular stock. The cases were opened and it was clearly visible that the contents were cigarettes marked," For export only". Mr. Alphenaar had no explanation for the cigarettes being commingled with his store inventory. Additionally 6 packages of Player light cigarettes and a broken carton of MacDonald cigarettes containing 10 packages were found commingled with the store cigarette inventory. None of these packages of cigarettes had Washington cigarette tax stamps affixed. There were 13 cases containing 25 cartons each of U.S. brand cigarettes, and 18 cases containing 50 cartons each of Canadian cigarettes. The total number of unbroken cartons of contraband cigarettes was 1225 or 10,450 packages of unstamped, untaxed cigarettes. Mr. Alphenaar contacted agents from the U.S. Custom service and advised him the Mr. Hess had called him and would be coming to Point Roberts on the morning of December 2, 1992 to pick up his cases of "circulars", the code name given the cigarettes. On the morning of

December 2, 1992, the delivery service P.R.A.F. made a second controlled delivery to the liquor store of the remaining 15 cases of contraband cigarettes designated "circulars". Mr. Hess arrived at Point Roberts and cleared customs at 2:11 p.m. Mr. Hess went directly to the liquor store and loaded 11 cases into his car. He left the liquor store and was unloading the cases in Mr. Alphenaar's garage when he was arrested and the cigarettes and his vehicle was seized. Hess was advised of his Miranda rights, which he stated he understood and would waive. He was taken to the Port Office to await transportation to the Whatcom County Jail. Hess stated that Alphenaar knew of the contents of the cases stored in the liquor store stock room. Hess stated that he was the seller and Alphenaar was the buyer. Hess stated that his revenue projections of approximately $40,000 per month profit was based upon a standing order of 50 cases or 2500 cartons of cigarettes per month made by Alphenaar. Hess stated he came to Point Roberts to collect $25,000 Alphenaar owed him for the 30 cartons delivered November 24th and December 2 1992. Hess stated Alphenaar paid him approximately $10,000 in cash for earlier deliveries of cigarettes. Hess stated "all his transactions were made in cash!"

On the 31st day of March 1994, Paul Hess entered a guilty plea. He was able to reduce the felony conviction to a gross misdemeanor which carried a 365 day sentence all suspended and a fine in the amount of $2500.00. The jails in Whatcom County were full and Paul never spent one day in jail serving a sentence for this crime against the people of the State of Washington.

When Paul Hess actually abducted his own children and fled to Egypt with them in the early 80s, he was eventually extradited and sent back to the U.S., to stand trial. Newspapers around Kansas reported that their former Senator had fled the country when he was found engaged in theft in Kansas. In 1994, he was indicted for trafficking in illegal goods in Whatcom County. At first, the indictment was a felony, later dropped as he pleads guilty to a misdemeanor and fined a whopping $2,000.00. Hess was bringing in $40,000 a month; this was just the cost of doing business. Now Hess was looking at jail time again, a calculated risk for someone who checks into jail like we check into the Holiday Inn. The difference in our case is he wrapped himself up with Washington Attorneys.

CHAPTER 7

THE POLICE

The police arrived at the door of Price and Farrington. Mr. Price, who was also involved in the "bonus scheme", would not allow the police in the office. Price and Farrington recently became aware of Hess convictions. I showed up later and asked for the funds back and received part of the funds back in the amount of $29,689.90. I then went to Mr. Shaner and he returned part of the funds as well. I approached Ms. Angel and she returns all the funds. Most of the employees were in shock, and did not know where their next paycheck was coming from.

Another meeting took place where I went to demand the return of all of the funds. Paul, Glenn and Chuck were present. Paul claimed to have a cashier's check for $17,000 provided I sign a mutual settlement and release. I refused and Glenn became upset, so upset he shouted and started pounding the table with his fist, unlike him. Unfortunately, I grew up in the South and things like that bother me. When the pounding and shouting starts to take place, either fight or leave and I picked up my stuff and left. The Bellevue police were not helpful as they saw this to be a "civil" matter. The FBI would not get involved as the amount was too small. When I asked them about "too small" they said we usually do not get involved in embezzlement unless it is over $450,000. (Good to know).

Next, I met with John Carver, prosecuting attorney in Seattle and he said it looks to be 25% criminal and 75% civil and because of the civil nature, Glenn and Chuck were board members and Paul was an officer, they declined to prosecute.

Chapter 8

NO HELP

Not much to do except pick up the pieces. The Police were thwarted, the FBI would not get involved as the embezzlement was too small and they are fighting "homeland security". The Washington Courts were the only hope for resolution. A lawsuit was filed in January of 2004 for theft, conversion etc. Surely the courts will bring the funds back to the company, the rightful owner. Anyone can see the bank account has "badges of fraud" written all over it! I also sent the facts to the Washington Bar Association knowing that attorneys should not be involved in criminal activities. This was the first time I have ever filed a Bar complaint. Does the Washington Bar allow their attorneys to partner with convicted disbarred attorneys? I sent them the following statement:

Declaration of Nicholas Paleveda MBA J.D. LL.M, CEO PFP Plan Administrators, the 412iCompany.

I Nicholas Paleveda MBA J.D. LL.M CEO The 412i Company make this declaration regarding the embezzlement of $ 146,181.90 of corporate funds by Mr. Price, Farrington and Hess. I am an attorney licensed in good standing before the Florida Bar for 19 years without a client complaint. I am licensed before the U.S. Tax Court and 11th Circuit Court of appeals and I am the CEO of the 412i Company. Mr. Hess is a convicted felon with convictions for theft, forgery, securities fraud and trafficking in illegal goods. He was disbarred in 1984. Mr. Price and Farrington are members of the Washington Bar who worked closely with and assisted Mr. Hess in the embezzlement of corporate funds to benefit themselves in the amount of $43,000.00 and expected another $178,000.00 which the company stopped them from receiving.

On June 15, 2001 the Company PFP plan administrators was formed by Nicholas Paleveda who had a tax background and insurance background and good relationships attorneys around the U.S. Mr. Paleveda, Glenn Price and Charles Farrington local attorneys and Bill Faiferlick a local insurance agent formed the PFP Plan Administration company. Stock was issued in the following amount 37.5% to Nick Paleveda, 37.5% to Bill Faiferlick and 25% to Price and Farrington. In addition, 50% of the stock was held as Treasury stock. Mr. Paleveda was elected President and CEO of the Company and has held this office since the beginning of the company. The company PFP plan administrators also filed a d/b/a as The412icompany. The company administers 412(i) defined benefit plans for insurance companies.

On or about October 1, 2003 Paul R. Hess was retained to assist the reorganization of the company. Paul Hess had known Nick Paleveda the CEO of the company for 3 years. Mrs. Jan Hess told Mr. Paleveda that he was an attorney and a member of the Kansas Bar. Mr. Hess also made the statement he was an attorney and member of the Kansas Bar. This was all a big lie by Mr. Hess and Mrs. Hess. The fact is Mr. Hess was disbarred in

1984 and since 1984-1992 was convicted of
multiple felonies including forgery, securities fraud
and trafficking in illegal goods in 1992. Mr.
Paleveda was unaware of the convictions as some
of the convictions were expunged.

On or about November 1, 2002, the company was
reorganized giving Mr. Paleveda 82.5% of the stock,
Price and Farrington 12.5% of the stock and Mr.
Hess 2.5% of the stock.. Mr. Hess was invited to
join the company as a part time consultant on
November 1, 2003. Mr. Hess claimed that he had
been the COO for many other companies and as an
attorney would be available for the COO position at
the 412i Company.

On or about February 1, 2003 Mr. Paleveda asked
Mr. Hess to become the COO of the company and a
full time employee. Mr. Hess received a salary of
$85,000 per year and all the funds were
administered through Paychecks.

On March 7, 2003 Mr. Hess approached Mr.
Paleveda about a bonus structure. He said we
needed to give the employees an incentive to
continue working at the company. Mr. Paleveda
recognized the advantage to this and Mr. Hess
suggested .05% for Sharon Angel, .05% for Doug

Farrar, 2.5% for Erik Shaner and 8% for Mr. Hess. He explained the bonuses would be non-binding. Mr. Paleveda stated that the bonus structure needed to be non-binding. Mr. Hess presented a contract for himself at 8% which Mr. Paleveda refused to sign as the bonus if any could only be paid after the solvency of the company was assured. On or about March 11, 2003 Mr. Hess presented another contract to Mr. Paleveda regarding his own compensation package. Mr. Paleveda disagreed with certain parts of the arrangement and did not enter into a formal contract. Mr. Hess continued working for the $85,000 salary. In May 2003, the company started to earn funds and a bonus was paid to Charles Gramp the Chief Actuary in the amount of $17,000 as agreed to in his employment agreement. The bonus was paid earlier then expected. Mr. Hess continued to press for his "bonus" arrangement and was told on many occasions that the company had to meet certain minimums approximately $750,000 by June 30 2003 to discuss bonuses. The Salaries of the employees needed to be paid as well as rent and other expenses.

Mr. Hess did not like this answer but he understood and Mr. Hess continued employment. Mr. Hess then realized that a check in the amount of $146,181.90 was coming to the company. Mr. Hess then devised a scheme to open a separate bank account under the name PFP Plan administrators as the check was written to the company not to Charles Farrington who held the insurance license for the company but did not work actively on the cases. . Mr. Price and Mr. Farrington law practice was in bad financial shape and the golden opportunity to receive significant money came to them. Mr. Hess went to the board members Charles Farrington, and Glenn Price and convinced them they would not get paid well unless the money was seized and cashier's checks written to them. He also convinced Mr. Farrington that he could sign his name to two cases, the Minas case and the Ludeman case and receive commissions in the amount of $35,000 and $178,000 respectfully.

Mr. Hess then made up statements to Mr. Price and Mr. Farrington that the company was not being run correctly and Mr. Paleveda and Ms. Ewing were bad people. Mr. Price and Mr. Farrington did not work in the company, spent no time working at the company but were desperate for money. Mr. Price had complained to Mr. Paleveda that Price and Farrington were in the worse financial position in 10 years.

With no knowledge given to Mr. Paleveda
Mr. Hess Price and Farrington held a secret board
meeting to embezzle the funds. They even held an
illegal board meeting between the two of them to
approve of the embezzlement and did not notify Mr.
Paleveda. The embezzlement took place in secrecy
until all the cashier's checks were issued to
themselves-then then notified Mr. Paleveda. They
told Mr. Paleveda that we notified you so we would
not be arrested for embezzlement- as attorneys
they knew the law and that in Washington they
would not be arrested. Mr. Price said as a former
prosecutor he said "knew that the police would do
nothing. " Mr. Farrington on July 1, 2002 issued
himself an RGA contract. Mr. Farrington also
placed himself as agent of record on the Minas
case even though Mr. Farrington never met with
Mr. Minas and never worked on his company's
pension plan. Mr. Farrington then took the
$35,000.00 commission. On July 18th 2003 Mr.
Hess, Mr. Farrington, and Mr. Price seized the
check that was written to the 412iCompany in the
amount of $146,181.90. This check was written to
the company intended for payroll. Mr. Hess,
Farrington and Price knew this and wanted to
embezzle the funds for their own use. In order to
accomplish this goal they opened up a separate
bank account without the knowledge consent or

58

approval of the Board member, majority shareholder, CEO and President Nick Paleveda. They secretly deposited the check in the new bank account on 7/24/03 and secretly issued cashier's checks to themselves on 8/01/03 once they accomplished their embezzlement goals, they notified Mr. Paleveda on 8/8/03.

Mr. Hess, Price, and Farrington opened up a new bank account never used by the company, deposited the funds in the bank account and wrote cashier's checks to themselves in the amount of $77,608.00 to Mr. Hess $19,285 to Mr. Shaner, $13,336 to Mr. Price and Mr. Farrington and $3626 to Mr. Farrar, and $1774 to Mrs. Angel. Mr. Price, Farrington and Hess then all resigned from the company and tendered back their stock. Mr. Paleveda, the CEO of the company, Board member and 82.5% shareholder was unaware of all this until an e-mail was sent August 9th explaining what they did. Mr. Hess claimed, after the funds were embezzled, that the company was not being run properly and that he may not get his bonus so he embezzled it instead. Mr. Price and Mr. Farrington, whose law firm practice was in the worst financial shape in 10 years, made a deal with Mr. Hess to take $35,000 as the commission for a case they had no involvement and an additional $13,336.00 with the hope to take another commission of $117,000.00 to give them a grand total of $134,880.00. Mr. Hess showed Mr. Farrington how he could change the name on cases he never worked on from the company to his individual name and pocket a quick $35,000.00.

The following Monday August 11th, Mr. Paleveda then contacted the Bellevue Police department who discovered that Mr. Hess was charged in 1985 with two counts of felony theft in Kansas and pleaded guilty to one count of felony theft. Mr. Hess was not an attorney but disbarred in 1986. Mr. Paleveda was totally unaware of Mr. Hess having a criminal record or disbarment. Mr. Paleveda was always under the understanding that Mr. Hess was a member in good standing of the Kansas Bar and did not know about the convictions. Mr. Paleveda discovered that Mr. Hess had arrest and convictions in 1986, 1987, 1992 and 1994 including forgery, securities fraud, trafficking in illegal goods and taxes. Mr. Paleveda was totally unaware of his past convictions and shocked and dismayed not only about the embezzlement but the disbarment as well. When the police arrived at the door of Price and Farrington the lawyers Mr. Price, who was also involved in the embezzlement would not allow the police in the office. Mr. Paleveda showed up later and asked for the funds back and received a check for $29,689.90. Mr. Paleveda then went to Mr. Shaner and he returned part of the funds as well. Mr. Paleveda approached Ms. Angel and she stated that she would return the funds as soon as she receives them.

Mr. Hess refuses to return the funds, has threatened to turn the corporation over to the IRS if anything was made of the embezzlement even though all payroll taxes are up to date minus the funds embezzled by Mr. Hess, Mr. Price, Farrington and Farrar. Mr. Price and Farrington also refused to return all of the embezzled funds as well as Mr. Farrar who stated he had a "deal" with Mr. Hess and was going to keep the embezzled funds.

Mr. Paleveda filed a Bar complaint against Mr. Price and Mr. Farrington who defended saying "it was their fiduciary duty" to take the funds and give them to Mr. Hess Mr. Price and Farrington. Mr. Price produced an unsigned forged document. When Mr. Paleveda said the document was a forgery and unsigned Mr. Farrington replied "it doesn't matter we want the money." When Mr. Paleveda demanded the funds be returned to the company as the check was a corporate check Mr. Price got angry and upset and pounded on the table with his fist at which time Mr. Paleveda left and filed this complaint and the complaint to the

Bar which has been stayed pending the outcome of this matter.

_____

Nick Paleveda
Member of the Florida Bar #394505

Great letter to the Bar—but no help.

Chapter 9

ATTACK THY ACCUSER!

A good defense starts with a good offense. Glenn Price knew this and rounded up Paul Hess to make a demonizing attack. If the facts don't support this, make them up, ignore the issue and fire. Paul had learned as a politician, demonizing opponents is the way to go so...

 Instead of receiving a response to my complaint, Glenn Price orchestrated a demonizing attack on the person who filed the complaint which was me. Here was his reply to the bar.

To the Washington State Bar Association
Office of Disciplinary Counsel

November 3, 2003.
THE GRIVANT"S BACKGROUND,
CHARACTER AND PERSONAL HISTORY

"How can you treat people so poorly?"

We respectfully request that the Board of Disciplinary Counsel carefully consider the grievant' background, character and personal history (their "track Record") in evaluating the context and credibility of the accusations in their bar grievance. Your office's understanding of the background and context of this matter is material to your assessment of the facts and will assist you in concluding that the actions Charles Farrington and I took as officers and directors in good faith on behalf of the corporation we served were necessary to avoid the adverse consequences of the grievant' repeated pattern of behavior.

The facts underlying this grievance emerge from a very specific context. That context is the background, character and personal history of the grievant Paleveda and Ewing. They are a profoundly dysfunctional, co-dependent couple who shield themselves from their own inadequacies through a repeated pattern of behavior that leads them to exploit, manipulate and attack others. In targeting my partner and me as their latest victims, Paleveda and Ewing are also victimizing the Washington State Bar Association, as I discuss in Section VIII of this Declaration.

We know Paleveda and Ewing. We know them better since thoroughly investigating them in preparing our responses to these bar grievances. Paleveda and Ewing have left behind them a wide swath of deceived, disappointed and damaged people-former colleagues, clients, employees, business associates, agents, advisors, lessors, homeowners and others. Our experience with Paleveda and Ewing and our own investigation of their background and history reveals a repeated and continuing pattern of victimization of each of these groups. When serious accusations are leveled against honorable people, as Paleveda and Ewing have done in their grievance, the accusers had better have their facts and their character straight. In this instance, they have neither. Had we been aware of even a fraction of Paleveda and Ewing's past, we would have never, under any circumstances, have aligned our professional and personal fates with them in any capacity, under any circumstances.

The specific facts and chronology of events relating to our involvement with Paleveda and Ewing and the 412(i)Company are set forth in exhaustive detail in the material we have submitted to your office including the Farrington Declaration and Response, the Hess declaration and the many other statements and exhibits. Please refer to them for a detailed account of the facts underlying this grievance; the review of those facts is not the primary purpose if (sic) this declaration. The specific facts of this matter are, like a skeleton, bare and incomplete until clothed by the skin of Paleveda and Ewing's personal history and character only then do they fully emerge. To underscore the source of this grievance, you must first come to know who has brought it.

Paleveda and Ewing have crafted a consistent modus operandi-in their lives and in their business dealings-in which they abuse, manipulate and lie. They shield themselves from their own inadequacies by exploiting others. They burnish their own bad character by attacking the good reputation of others. That behavior is the basis for the filing of these grievances with your office. One would think that Paleveda and Ewing's recognition of their own vulnerabilities would make them more circumspect about how they conduct their business affairs and relationships. One would think that Paleveda and Ewing's history of dishonest and unethical behavior would have given them pause before filing this grievance. But they are not circumspect. They are reckless. They attack. While the consequences of their actions create a turbulent wake, they are oblivious to those consequences. They see only as far as their latest "grievance", their last "slight", and they look to manipulate the first available agency or authority they can find to carry out their personal vendettas cost-free. As one former employee of The412(i)Company said: "How can you treat people so poorly?"(See Shaner Statement,Ex. 20).

"Like most of Mr. Paleveda's promises, he never delivered."

"He caused me a lot of harm"

"Why don't you try integrity?"

The facts of this case arise from a destructive disconnect between Paleveda's and Ewing's view of money and ethics. Paleveda and Ewing have gained and lost substantial money over the years as a result of their self-sabotaging lifestyle. A former colleague of his describes Paleveda receiving large insurance commissions in the past and Ewing's mismanagement of the money: "Marjorie would get a huge infusion of cash, spend it and go into debt." Paleveda has told me that Ewing "is not good with money", and that when he was in the insurance business, he would have credit card bills of $20,000.00 per month from Ewing's spending habits."

The attack harangued on and on accusing "Paleveda and Ewing" for such deeds as "moving around" to disputes with landlords. Glenn Price and Paul Hess mastermind this attack based upon their own problems. Glenn Price had engaged in a lawsuit with his former supplier of legal forms AEP and had sued automobile companies, moved around a lot himself, even going to Saipan. What facts they did not know, they made up-if you do not like the truth-make it up! This served them well throughout the arbitration, motion hearing, pleadings etc.

The Washington Bar comment was-it is OK to lie if you believe it is true.-Or put it bluntly, there is no real "perjury" in civil court. However, it its best to have your lawyer lie for you-as he or she may be immune from process where you could end up in trouble.

With no knowledge given to me, Hess Price and Farrington held a secret board meeting, which I was not invited and even made a statement that stated I was not invited. The problem is this is against corporate law to have a secret meeting and not invite the majority shareholder and board member, but then again this is the wild west of Washington and we are in front of a "neutral" arbitrator. What would a "neutral" arbitrator think of a secret board meeting in violation of state law? **

** (Under Washington law it is clear that board members need to be notified for a special meeting see RCW 48.17.490.-the rule makes sense otherwise chaos would exist and board meetings could be held without all board members present anytime.)

We argued the defendants held an illegal board meeting between the two of them to approve of the embezzlement and did not notify me, the majority owner and board member. The embezzlement took place in secrecy until all the cashier's checks were issued to themselves-then

then notified me. (Price and Farrington told me that they needed to notify me otherwise they could be convicted of embezzlement according to their legal research). They told me that I was notified you so they would not be arrested for embezzlement- as attorneys they knew the law and that in Washington they would not be arrested. Mr. Price said as a former prosecutor he said "knew that the police would do nothing."

Mr. Farrington also revoked the corporate licenses and placed himself as agent of record on all the cases. Mr. Farrington then took a $35,000.00 commission personally that was due to the company. On July 18th 2003 Mr. Hess, Mr. Farrington, and Mr. Price seized the check that was written to The 412(i)Company in the amount of $146,181.90. This check was written to the company intended for payroll. Mr. Hess, Farrington and Price knew this and wanted to embezzle the funds for their own use. In order to accomplish this goal they opened up a separate bank account without the knowledge consent or approval of the Board member, majority shareholder, CEO and President Nick Paleveda. They secretly deposited the check in the new bank account on 7/24/03 and secretly issued cashier's checks to themselves on 8/01/03 once they accomplished their embezzlement goals, they notified Mr. Paleveda on 8/8/03.

Mr. Hess, Price, and Farrington new bank account was only used for the embezzlement. They deposited the funds in the bank account and wrote cashier's checks to themselves in the amount of $77,608.00 to Mr. Hess $19,285 to Mr. Shaner, $13,336 to Mr. Price and Mr. Farrington and $3,626 to Mr. Farrar, and $1,774 to Mrs. Angel. Mr. Price, Farrington and Hess then all resigned from the company and tendered back their stock. Mr. Paleveda, the CEO of the company, Board member and 82.5% shareholder was unaware of all this until an e-mail was sent August 9th explaining what they did.

Mr. Hess claimed, after the funds were embezzled, that the company was not being run properly and that he may not get his bonus so he embezzled it. Mr. Price and Mr. Farrington, whose law firm practice was in the worst financial shape in 10 years, made a deal with Mr. Hess to take $35,000 as the commission for a case they had no involvement and an additional $13,336.00 with the hope to take another commission of $117,000.00 to give them a grand total of $134,880.00. Mr. Hess showed Mr. Farrington how he could change the name on cases he never worked on from the company to his individual name and pocket a quick $35,000.00.

CHAPTER 10

LAW FIRM RESICK HANSEN AND FOLLIS

No help there so I turned to Resick Hansen and Follis, a law firm in Bellingham.

I explained the story to Tom Resick.

" The police went to arrest Mr. Hess but were stopped at the door of the Law Firm of Price and Farrington. Glenn Price, being a former prosecutor knew the rules and explained to the police it was a "business dispute" and asked the police to leave.... which they did".

I entered the office of Price and Farrington. Hess made his way into the room after the police had left. Price explained how unhappy they were with the move of the company up to Bellingham and the reasons they took the accounts to pay themselves bonuses.

Price and Farrington explained they convened a board meeting and did not invite Nick to pass a resolution authorizing the bank account and bonuses to be paid to themselves. Hess convinced Farrington that he could sign his name to two pension case and receive commissions in the amount of $35,000 and $117,000 respectfully. The takeover was a success!

Paul had then devised a scheme to open a secret bank account in Bellevue under the name PFP Plan administrators but needed some assistance which he found from Charles Farrington. Hess convinced Mr. Farrington that he could assure tens of thousands of dollars perhaps hundreds of thousands of dollars could be diverted into Price Farrington and Hess's account and that Nick and Marjorie are up to no good. Hess told Price and Farrington that all Nick and Marjorie would do with the funds is pay employees and rent and they would benefit not Price and Farrington.

Hess convinced Farrington to open a secret bank account in the name of the company, which deposit the check and issue cashier's checks to themselves, and if Nick and Marjorie did not cooperate, pull the insurance license from the company!

This seemed like a good idea to Glenn and Chuck, why should this money go to the employees? A secret bank account was opened by Farrington. Unfortunately, Farrington had not really been involved in the company so on the bank application listed the company as an S corporation(when it really was a C) he listed 1 employee (when there was really 7) and listed himself as the only key employee. Nevertheless, the account was opened, the stage was set. Hess then called the insurance company and diverted the check that was written to PFP Plan Administrators from Bellingham to Bellevue and into the secret bank account! Now they waited until the checks cleared an issued each Hess Price and Farrington cashier's checks! This was all done without the knowledge and consent of Nick the CEO and majority shareholder, the employees of the company until August 8, 2003."

Resick Hansen and Follis is your typical small town law firm where attorneys work in the courthouse on a daily basis. The "real" attorneys are found in firms like these as they daily deal with matters before the court. Tom Resick was an experience trial attorney with many years of court room experience. Tom had even served as a judge in Whatcom County. "Have a seat", Tom said as he stood up to pace back and forth. "I like to pace while I listen to your story". I told him the facts, his eyes widen in disbelief," They are attorneys?" he said. "Well, I though they all were, one turned out to be a disbarred convicted felon". "We need to find out more about this guy Hess, I am going to bring a P.I. to review the situation" Tom said. Our next meeting was with the P.I. who took the data and started investigating Paul. He came up with numerous complaints and convictions against Paul.

Tom Resick's name was given to me by Steve Moore, our friendly realtor. Tom had been an attorney in Bellingham for years and knew his was in and out of the courtroom. His office was in a converted house near the courtroom which is quite popular for attorneys who practice before judges on a daily basis. Tom agreed to handle the case and filed suit against Hess, Price and Farrington.

When the complaint was filed, a motion to move to arbitration came back signed by Eric Zimbelman. The name sounded familiar and a court date was set before Judge Nichols. Into the courtroom walked Eric Zimbelman.

The Law Firm of Peel Brimley is located in a seedy part of Seattle. Generally it is difficult to find a "seedy" part in Seattle, but if there was one, Peel Brimley had found it. The offices once you arrived safely were nicely appointed. Once you stepped out of the office panhandlers would come up and ask for money.

Now if there was a definition for a "bulldog attorney" Eric would fit the bill. Relentless, cunning and reckless, Eric went for the win at every stage of the proceedings. Truth is dammed, full speed ahead! Eric immediately asked for sanctions against Tom for now withdrawing a motion soon enough in violation of Washington law yadda-yadda.

We opposed the motion to remove to arbitration even though there was an arbitration agreement in our licensing and technology agreement because this case had nothing to do with licensing, it was corporate theft! Judge Nichols would here none of that and ordered the parties to arbitration in Seattle.

Tom was non-plussed. Seattle in arbitration, he doesn't do that. It would be like asking an attorney in Des Monies to handle arbitration in New York City or Miami. Tom wanted us to get someone else; he was not going to Seattle. The emerald city on the outside had something else lurking on the inside which outsiders just don't understand. In any event, we had to go to Seattle for the arbitration and we were resigned to this fate. IS Seattle the legal sewer of the Northwest, I could not be sure but it could not be worse than Miami or New York where I had worked. I had not been to arbitration in years, but what I had done in mediation in Florida worked out real good for the parties. AAA or the American Arbitration Association was supposed to be the best. We would have a good "neutral" arbitrator who could listen to this and the cosmic order of the universe would be re-aligned. Arbitration is purported to be "less expensive" then mediation...until you review the arbitrators. We filed for arbitration, a $3,000 filing fee. Wait a minute court is only $250.00? We reviewed the list of arbitrators, all white male over age 50. I guess there are no qualified women or blacks arbitrators in Washington. We need an attorney to represent us so we hired a recent graduate Jesse Haas who had just graduated from University of Oregon and had some experience in litigation matters, but this was just an arbitration/mediation and the last one I went to the cost was about $300.00 and it was informal and the mediators were good, real good but that was in Florida.

But this is Washington.

Mr. Hess refuses to return the funds, has threatened to turn the corporation over to the IRS if anything was made of the embezzlement. These threats were in writing and entered into evidence and ignored by Mr. Easter in his "reasoned opinion". Mr. Price and Farrington also refused to return all of the embezzled funds as well as Mr. Farrar who stated he had a "deal" with Mr. Hess and was going to keep the embezzled funds.

Mr. Paleveda filed a Bar complaint against Mr. Price and Mr. Farrington who defended saying "it was their fiduciary duty" to take the funds and give them to Mr. Hess Mr. Price and Farrington. Mr. Price produced an unsigned document to support Mr. Hess. When Mr. Paleveda said the document was a forgery and unsigned Mr. Farrington replied "it doesn't matter we want the money." When Mr. Paleveda demanded the funds be returned to the company as the check was a corporate check Mr. Price got angry and upset and pounded on the table with his fist at which time Mr. Paleveda left and filed a complaint to the Bar, and a civil action. The Bar complaint has been stayed pending the outcome of this matter.

The Superior Court of Whatcom County ordered the case to Arbitration even though the case fell outside the "Licensing and Technology Agreement" which did not cover corporate disputes or insurance contract law.

Chapter 11

The "Neutral" Arbitrator Scott Easter of Montgomery Purdue Blankenship and Austin

"Are there any qualified female arbitrators in the State of Washington?"

The American Arbitration Association is the pride of Arbitration associations in the United States. The arbitrators are well educated, senior, intelligent neutrals who act as surrogate judges to take the burden off of the traditional legal system. But arbitration has changed since the 70's when I went with Dr. Sherman, a professor at the University of South Florida, to witness arbitration in Orlando. His fee back then was $300.00. Today the application fee was $3,000.00 and the annual hourly rates averaged $300.00 per hour.

When the list was sent to us, we reviewed each name carefully. We were looking to strike arbitrators who would have a bias against our client. We were also looking for arbitrators who may be more favorable. Since our client was a woman, naturally we would like a female arbitrator. In Washington, there were no female arbitrators. "Jesse, Are there any females qualified to be arbitrators in the State of Washington?" I asked. No minorities were qualified either-all the choices were white male over age 50." I guess the AAA doesn't believe in diversity in this state." This appeared quite irregular in a state that has a female Governor, two female senators and is suppose to be "progressive". There are even female judges-but no qualified female arbitrators. We were about to walk head first into the good old boy network that dominates Washington state.

Montgomery Purdue Blankenship and Austin is the law firm Scott Easter is a partner. The law firm bills itself as

"A full service law firm providing business, real estate. Estate planning and legal litigation services. MPBA has been in existence since 1912. We successfully maintain a loyal client base and we believe that there is no business law firm in the State of Washington of comparable size that is better respected in our legal community. We are committed to ethical practice and the highest quality of work."

The law firm is located in the tallest building in Seattle, the Columbia tower, now known as the Bank of America Building, but old habits die slowly in Seattle and everyone knows the building as the "Columbia tower". Rising nearly 1000 feet into the air it is one of the largest buildings in the U.S. and the view from the top is fabulous. Only in this "tower of power" would law firms like Montgomery Purdue exist. This was to be the setting for the arbitration. Jesse Hass would represent the company and Erik Zimbelman would represent the defendants. It was a clear open shut case. The problem as any lawyer knows, proving the case may be a different matter.

In Arbitration the plaintiffs and defendants have to rely on the neutrality of the arbitrator as any appeal is limited. The neutrality of the arbitrator gives confidence in the legal system and the parties have an opportunity to review the resumes of the arbitrators to prevent any possible bias. The American Arbitration Association sent us a list of perhaps a dozen arbitrators. All of the choices were White Male over age 40 or 50. I wondered if in Seattle any qualified females or African Americans existed. Unfortunately our client was a female and there was no choice but to pick a white male arbitrator. Justice is supposed to be color blind, but the American Arbitration Association choices may have reflected the Seattle community-all white males. How can this be? Are there no white females who are qualified in Washington? The do represent 50% of the population. I remember an old television program "Here come the brides" where women were transported to Seattle to become brides as there was a lack of available women in Seattle. Could this be true in 2003, a lack of qualified women candidates? In any event Jesse Hass our counsel for the arbitration and I went through the list. This person graduated from Harvard, strike him, because Glenn graduated from Harvard and there may be some bias toward a fellow graduate. This person lived in Bellevue, strike him possible bias. This one looks good, he went to Stanford and works for a small law firm in Seattle, Montgomery Purdue Blankenship and Austin. The American Arbitration Association then gave a list of 14 attorneys which both parties selected

Scott B. Easter of Montgomery Purdue Blankenship and Austin. A phone meeting was held prior to the arbitration. During the phone appointment, Mr. Easter assured the parties of a conflict check and that he and his firm had no relationship with the defendants or the plaintiffs. He sent the conflict check to the American Arbitration Association. We were comfortable that he and his firm had no relationship past or present with any of the parties. His conflict check even mentioned some of his partners that had run into some of our attorneys at prior hearings. We felt we had a safe and reliable arbitrator. We first met Scott Easter though a telephone conference where he disclosed that he had no knowledge of the parties and his neutrality could be assured. Jess Hass had been retained as our corporate counsel, as this was arbitration and the cause of action was quite clear.

When Jesse asked about a procedural issue, Scott snapped back, "I am not going to practice law for you counselor". But, he seemed independent which is all you want and knowledgeable about the law what more could one ask for from an arbitrator. In Florida, I had been before several arbitrators as Florida required court appointed mediation. The results were quite good and quite fair, which is all one, can ask. The arbitration was to take place in the office of Montgomery Purdue

Chapter 12

The Arbitration

"He was paid to do a job..."

The Arbitration hearing started in Seattle on October 31, 2005. We went down to Seattle from Bellingham to testify. The arbitration went well. We presented our case which is quite compelling, our attorney Paul Hess who also operated as our COO had along with Charles Farrington a local attorney had opened up a secret bank account and deposited a check of $149,000.00 into the account. Next, they issued cashier's checks to themselves-all having "Badges of Fraud" written all over it. The bank account had fraudulently stated the company was an "S" when it was a "C". The application said one employee when there was "7" and the sole shareholder was Charles Farrington when there were 4 shareholders. The total gross revenue was listed as $30,000.00 and he was depositing a $149,000.00 check. Nonetheless Well Fargo, whom Mr. Farrington had a prior relationship with, opened up the account. Clearly just plain old "Bank Fraud".

The Law Firm of Fahlman and Olsen is located on the waterfront in Seattle. Erik Fahlman was a local estate planning attorney who had an ax to grind with me as we did not allow his client to set up a defined benefit plan once we discovered his income was not from an active trade or business. Hess had called relationships of mine across the U.S. asking for any dirt, or would they testify or make statements etc. and hit a nerve with Erik Fahlman. Erik was brought in to impeach my credibility even though the arbitrator stated earlier that impeachment witnesses were not allowed. Erik blasted me and the arbitrator allowed it. He stated Bar complaints were filed against me by his clients and I was made out to be a charlatan. When we confronted Erik with evidence from the Bar that a complaint was not filed, he said "Oh Yes they filed it, I am sure they told me so." I just cannot find a copy of the complaint."

Erik Falhman, a local estate planning attorney testified for the defendant Hess stating bar complaints was filed against Nick Paleveda by his clients. (This was later proven to be not true.) I then did file a Bar complaint against Mr. Fahlman for lying at the arbitration (but Mr. Fahlman was allowed to lie as he is an attorney) and my complaint was dismissed.

Chapter 13

Watch the Arbitrator (Maybe I am not a neutral arbitrator!)

In the middle of the Arbitration, confident that we would be the prevailing party as the defendant clearly was guilty of theft; we sent Marjorie Ewing to research the deeds at the County Courthouse. Marjorie came back with the deeds. One was Glenn Price placing a $50,000.00 line of credit on his house, perhaps to pay for the arbitration. The next deed was Charles Farrington's houses in Sammamish and the final deed was Paul Hess, whose house had been owned by Montgomery Purdue Blankenship and Austin who was the "trustee" for the Hess's what!? We were in shock. How could he be the "neutral arbitrator" and their attorney at the same time? It is things like this that destroy the integrity of the legal system. Mr. Easter's law firm was on the Hess payroll and we were litigating against Hess. When you see stuff like this, any moron will know that it is wrong. How can you be a "neutral" arbitrator when the person who is the defendant is your former client who paid you to do a job? In fact, it may be unethical to rule against your client. We went back to Bellingham and after researching the proper procedure, we asked the AAA to release us from Mr. Easter and they refused. How can they refuse this request?

Scott Easter had a decision to make. He had a relationship with Mr. Zimbleman which he did not disclose on his original application but later disclosed this and we made a big error and waived it. Scott Easter also had a former client as the defendant in an arbitration and he took the arbitration pretending to be neutral. It is clear that arbitrators would become bias toward the attorneys who continued to bring the arbitrator cases.

Scott Easter sat in his office on the 42d floor of the Columbia tower with a decision to make. How could he go against an attorney who sends his firm business? How can he go against the defendant who was his firm's client? The firm had just moved to expensive new offices and the plaintiff's were from Bellingham 90 miles to the north. Politically if they were shafted it would mean nothing to him. Economically and politically helping out the Bellevue bandits would serve his cause.

The arbitrator has governing power over law and fact. In this case Scott knew he could ignore the law, brush off the facts and make an award in favor of his friendly attorney and his firm's client-and that is what he did. Politics would triumph over law and fact. After all, Scott did not know that we had seen the deeds with his firm's name splattered all over them along with Paul Hess. If the award was great enough, Scott knew the company could not recover and fight his firm, a firm entrenched in Seattle politics so deep in fact one of the partners of the firm served as head of the Washington Bar association at one time.

THE AWARD

There is really no need to go to law school and study the law if people like Mr. Easter are the decision makers. He did not either know the law, nor did he follow it and in many cases just ignored it. Perhaps he was "paid to do a job". What they do not tell law students in Washington is 80% of your practice is who you know, 20% is "What you know". Let's look at Mr. Easter's award.

FINAL REASONED AWARD.

Easter's first two statements regarding Prehearing stipulations and Rulings were not something even he could mess up.

3. Findings by the arbitrator.

3.1 Corporate formalities Not Followed. Clamant carried the burden of proof in establishing that the Washington statutes and the by-laws of the Company were not followed in the setting of the July 24, 2003 special board meeting.

In English, Price and Farrington could not hold a backdated board meeting without Nick being present and award themselves $145,000.00.
He got this one right!

3.2 Board action justified by Exigent Circumstances. Respondent have sustained their burden of proof in establishing that exigent circumstances

97

existed to justify their failure to follow normal procedures contained in Washington statutes and in the by-laws of the Company for the setting of a special board meeting on July 24, 2003. Such exigent circumstances included but were not limited to a pattern of behavior by Mr. Paleveda and Ms. Ewing disregarding normal corporate requirements including numerous examples of disregard of the corporate form, mismanagement and inappropriate diversion of corporate funds and assets as well as intermingling of corporate assets and personal assets. In general, corporate formalities were not observed by and largely ignored by all parties leading up to and including the July and August 2003 special board meeting.

Easter did not cite one example. The reason why is there was no example to cite. In fact we were following corporate procedure and his friends and clients were not.

This is where Easter starts violating the law. You can tell through his entire opinion when he wants to violate the law, he starts using buzz words such as "exigent Circumstances". This has meaning in criminal law but no place in a corporate boardroom. "exigent circumstances" usually is found in criminal law where actions are taken by police in the event of an emergency. Here, there is no emergency other than Hess want to take the money, but then again Hess is his client. Any partially competent attorney will know there is no room in corporate boardrooms for "exigent circumstances". For instance, if Disney were to have meetings with two directors and ignore the rest due to "exigent circumstances", their disputes would never be hashed out in the corporate boardrooms. Chaos would exist as anyone or two directors would make decisions and ignore the rest. There are no "life and death" situations made in corporate boardrooms that could ignore a director intentionally. Mr. Easter obviously never took a basic corporate law course.

3.3 Existence of Bonus Plan established.

Respondents establish by a preponderance of the evidence that a bonus plan had been established by the Company and continued up to and including July of 2003. Testimony by Mr. Paleveda and Ms. Ewing (and to some degree by Mr. Gramp) was not credible in disputing the existence of such a plan, nor did Claimant carry its burden of proof in establishing that such a plan violated then existing insurance statutes. Even if the claimant had establish a violation of insurance statutes under the doctrine of *in parit delecto,* Claimant would have been estopped or precluded as a matter of law form asserting such a defense to enforcement of the bonus plan.

Once again the law phase appears and once again Mr. Easter decides to violate Washington law. You cannot have insurance commissions split between non-licensed personnel. This was made clear in the Washington statute and is basic insurance law. Finally, Mr. Easter ignored state Insurance law allowing Mr. Farrington to split insurance commissions with non-licensed agents-Mr. Price and Mr. Hess etc. This is a clear violation of RCW 48.17.490. Mr. Easter said we did not prove our case. He stated our testimony was not credible (even though he had a signed statement from Hess Price and Farrington that they were splitting commissions). He also stated that we would be estopped by the doctrine of "in pari delicto" (I think Mr. Easter uses Latin phrases to impress or confuse his audience). This is clearly not the law in Washington State. The Arbitrator cannot enforce an illegal contract. Why would he agree to such an arrangement?

Mr. Farrington was reprimanded by the insurance commissioner. Mr. Easter obviously did not take a basic insurance course and once again violated Washington law. Violations on Easter 2-correct law 0.The bonus plan consisted of Mr. Hess's statement and a document signed by Hess allowing himself to be given a bonus with an unsigned place for Nick's signature. However, Easter needed to figure out some way to take care of his client and "in pari delecto" sounded confusing. Latin for "in equal fault" which means that two or more people are guilty of a crime neither can collect damages.

Mr. Easter then awarded the defendant Mr. Hess and associates nearly $100,000.00. Mr. Easter in his "reasoned opinion" stated our witnesses were "not credible". (-and Mr. Hess was?) I was insulted. Mr. Easter placed his belief and trust in Mr. Hess, who lied about his marriage to Jan Hess (we discovered that he was not married to her at the arbitration). He trusted Paul Hess who was a disbarred convicted felon who lied about his membership in the Kansas Bar and found our team not to be "credible". No written evidence supported Mr. Hess. Why would Mr. Easter rule in his favor? Res Ipsa Loquitur-or "the thing speaks for itself"- Mr. Hess is Mr. Easter's client-how could he rule against his client.

Mr. Easter in his reasoned opinion (see attached) denied my seat on the board of directors due to "exigent circumstances". The law is clear, my seat cannot be denied. If this was the law in any jurisdiction it would create corporate chaos. If the Easter rule was allowed to prevail, anytime a board wants to convene and did not want another party to attend the meeting the members could claim "exigent circumstances". Any first year law student knows this is basic corporate law. Why would Mr. Easter ignore Washington law? Res Ipsa Loquitur- Mr. Hess is Mr. Easter's client.

Res Ipsa Loquitur-he has a relationship with the Hess family.
We do not know how deep the Hess family relationship is with Scott Easter. We do know that checks came to the office of Montgomery Purdue from the Hess family or Joos/Hess every month for at least 3 years while Scott Easter was a partner in the firm. We can only suspect Hess had additional relationship with the firm Montgomery Purdue. Why?

Prior to the embezzlement Mr. Hess conducted secret meetings with Mr. Price, Mr. Farrington our chief actuary Mr. Gramp and our employee Sharon Angel. Ms. Angel and Mr.Gramp told us about those meetings. Mr. Price and Farrington made it clear they were meeting secretly with Mr. Hess in the arbitration. Mr. Hess has admitted in the past to make and receive cash payments in the amount of $10,000 to $24,000.00 in his convictions in Whatcom County. We have no assurances that this did not take place with Mr. Easter or his firm.

It would take a year and a federal subpoena to discover the 324 pages of correspondence between Hess and Montgomery Purdue, a relationship that lasted for 19 months while Montgomery Purdue had title to the Hess family home- all hidden by Mr. Easter who admitted later that he knew about this relationship, he just didn't want to disclose It.-Duh- Easter knew if he disclosed this relationship we would have been forced to find a real "neutral" arbitrator, one whose firm had not collected fees and had a relationship with the defendant. Easter had masked that he "did his due diligence" by listing other contacts his law firm had with our former attorney Tom Resick, but

never let on he had on his desk 324 pages
supplied to him by his own firm
Montgomery Purdue. The Law firm gave
him the conflicts list; he just chose to
ignore it.

Chapter 14

The County Judge

Preston Gates and Ellis is one of the largest law firms in the Pacific Northwest. Bill Gate's father actually started the firm and recently they merged with Kirkpatrick Lockhart to form one of the largest firms in the U.S. We contacted Preston Gates after Perkins Coie; another large Seattle law did not return any e-mails. Preston Gates had a stellar reputation in Seattle and we were put in contact with one of their top appellate attorneys Paul Lawrence. "What happened" said Paul. I explained the story. "Well arbitrators can have their way with the law, he said." What about manifest disregard for the law". I asked. "Tough to argue, better is what were you doing in arbitration in the first place?" The court sent us to arbitration. Paul did not think the case belonged in arbitration, there were too many unsigned agreements and the agreement that had an arbitration clause had nothing to do with our case, it referred to a licensing agreement. "This should never been in arbitration" he said. Preston Gates agreed to take the case. At last, we had someone with a clear knowledge of the law; however the bills kept mounting $20,000, $40,000, $60,000. No wonder the large law firms only handle large clients. At last the day of reckoning before Judge Snyder. Surely he could see this should not be before an arbitrator, especially where the arbitrator's law firm had a conflict that they did not disclose. I mean, the law firmed owned Paul's house for 19 months, there cannot be a cozier relationship then that unless one of their attorneys slept there. All the employees attended the hearing as the fate

of the company depended on the outcome.
15 people would lose their jobs if Judge
Snyder did not rule in our favor.

Judge Snyder listened to arguments
from the attorneys. 'Conflict of Interest?"
just because a law firms name shows up
on a deed, that doesn't mean a conflict."
he said

"You think it should not be in
arbitration, wait a minute, Judge Nichols
when he was on the bench, he ruled the
case belonged in arbitration, I am not
going to overturn that, case dismissed." he
said.

We asked the Whatcom Superior Court
to vacate the Judgment and it was denied.
Judge Charles Snyder had sat on the
bench for less than a year. He was to hear
arguments from one of the best attorney's
in Seattle at Preston Gates Paul Lawrence
against Eric Zimbelman a "bulldog"
attorney who doesn't mind bending the
truth especially when it suits his case.

(The rubber stamp of arbitration was placed on this case). We planned to appeal the case. The 9th circuit has already ruled in (*Schmitz v. Zilveti* 20 F.3d. 1043 9th Circuit 1994) that this type of conflict must be disclosed or the arbitration vacated-The 11th Circuit has also not allowed this type of skullduggery in *Positive Software v. New Century Mortgage* (7th Cir, 2006) -** and for good reason or it promotes a lack of integrity in the judicial system. We had no opportunity to question Mr. Easter about the nature and extent of the conflict. In my opinion Mr. Easter has no credibility.

** The 11th Circuit reverses this opinion in an "en-banc" proceeding later on during that year overturning their own three judge decision.

In the meantime Mr. Hess has a judgment against the company and Mr. Easter walks away. Hess has already garnished the company's profit sharing plan-illegal under Federal law but what is to stop him. The company subsequently filed for Federal Bankrupcy protection from these Washington lawyers. Subsequently we also discovered that Mr. Hess was responsible for the destruction of several local start-ups including Seminar Master, Q-Pharma and he almost destroyed Edvita, but the CEO dismissed him from the company on discovering child pornography on Hess's computer. We do not want this to happen again. It may be too late for our company, but we want to prevent Mr. Easter from doing damage to another company or individual. In the interest of justice we ask that he be permanently removed as an arbitrator. In the meantime proceed to "Plan B".

The company did not have the funds to "bond' an appeal. The company was broke after all the money was "bonus" and now the bad guys ran up a $140,000 legal bill and their friendly arbitrator asked the company to pay for it. Time to seek protection from the Federal Courts, or the Federal Bankruptcy Courts. Preston Gates referred us to Shelly Crocker, a bankruptcy specialist in Seattle,

Croker Kuno and Ostrovsky 's website states the firm "creates solutions for financially troubled companies and individuals....this appears to be the place for us. After having Paul Hess embezzle $146,000.00 and his lawyer Scott Easter award him another $100,000 in attorney's fees the company was definitely "financially troubled". Shelly Crocker was the lead attorney in the Firm and she met with Marjorie to file the bankruptcy petition. I had lost my interest in the firm after the first embezzlement and had no ownership rights at the time. I did research embezzlement and discovered that white collar crime was a 300-600 Billion dollar industry in the U.S. as opposed to regular crime which was a 1-2 billion dollar industry. I had no idea it was so large, but not surprising. Reams of papers were filled out listing all the assets and creditors of the company. In the meantime Zimbelman continued his rampage through state court flooding the court with garnishment proceedings and attachment.

Chapter 15

The Bar Association

The Washington Bar Association is responsible for maintaining the ethical conduct of its members. In the legal profession, the State Bar Associations are responsible for the conduct of its members. The Florida Bar News on December 15, 2007 made the following announcement. A lawyer refused to accept a check for satisfaction of judgment from another lawyer because it was 23 cents short-even after the lawyer reached into his pocket for a quarter to settle up. During a trial, a lawyer angrily talked back to a judge referring to him as "Judge Glare". In a deposition, a lawyer claimed she couldn't find a relevant document in her briefcase even though it was there among her papers-All three Florida lawyers were suspended from practicing law. Now the onus is on you and other members of the Bar to advertise decisions like that so lawyers know this is behavior is not tolerated!-stated the Florida Bar....but this is Washington....

After looking at Price and Farrington's involvement with Paul Hess, and reviewing the bank account which fraudulently issued cashier's checks to themselves, I filed a Bar compliant with the Washington Bar Association against both Glenn Price and Charles Farrington. It was clear to me that attorneys cannot engage in such "money laundering". The response by Mr. Beitel, counsel for the Washington Bar Association, was the matter would be "stayed" pending the outcome of the litigation. This is actually normal although it did spark a voluminous response from Glenn and Chuck who ballyhooed how "bad" I was and how "evil" Marjorie was and created enormous personal attacks some downright funny. The first rule lawyers learn in law school is-you're not guilty! Most criminals convict themselves by admitting guilt, but not the lawyer! Instead, attack your accuser and do not admit guilt! This is the defense Price and Farrington put on to the Washington Bar and was the hallmark of their deceit in years to follow.

I had never reported any attorney or registered any bar complaint in 23 years; this was to be my first. I filed a complaint against Price and Farrington for participating in the embezzlement, later I filed against Eric Fahlman for lying to the arbitrator and finally I filed a complaint against Scott Easter for operating as an arbitrator or as a "neutral" when he knew that his law firm had operated as trustee for the Hess family and in fact owned their home for 19 months prior to the arbitration and did not disclose this fact. In reading Scott Easter's "opinion" Scott had to violate no less than 3 clearly defined Washington state laws to rule in his client's favor.

1. He had to rule that a board meeting could take place without inviting certain board members that do not agree with your position.

2. He had to allow splitting insurance commissions with a non-licensed individual.

3. He had to allow a company to go insolvent by paying bonus money to insiders.

Here is a copy of the complaint.

Complaint regarding Scott B. Easter of Montgomery, Purdue, Blankenship, and Austin PLLC acting as a Judicial Arbitrator in the case 412(i) Company v. Hess et.al.

I, Nicholas Paleveda MBA J.D. LL.M and former CEO of The 412(i) Company member of the Florida Bar Association for over 22 years without a client complaint, make this complaint against Scott B

Easter, Judicial Arbitrator regarding the hidden legal and financial relationship between Scott B. Easter of Montgomery, Purdue, Blankenship and Austin and Paul and Jan Hess the primary defendants in the arbitration.

The case involves the embezzlement of $ 146,181.90 of corporate funds by Mr. Hess, who obtained employment at The412iCompany by presenting himself as an attorney and member of the Kansas Bar. The case involves a distinct class attorneys.

Nick Paleveda MBA J.D. LL.M. an attorney licensed in good standing before the Florida Bar since 1984 without a client complaint. I am licensed before the U.S. Tax Court and 11th Circuit Court of appeals. I was the CEO of the 412(i) Company during the time of the arbitration.

Mr. Hess J.D., after the embezzlement of the funds, was discovered to be a convicted felon with convictions for theft, forgery, securities fraud and trafficking in illegal goods. He was disbarred in 1984. He was an attorney in Kansas and a Kansas state senator and state house member.

Mr. Price J.D. and Farrington J.D. LL.M are members of the Washington Bar who worked closely with and assisted Mr. Hess in the embezzlement of corporate funds to benefit themselves in the amount of $43,000.00 (and expected another $178,000.00 which the company stopped them from receiving.)

Mr. Erik Fahlman J.D. a local estate planning attorney who lied and slandered Mr. Paleveda at the arbitration on behalf of Hess and Price.

Mr. Scott Easter J.D. was the "neutral" arbitrator in this case acting as a judicial officer who did not disclose that the defendants Mr. and Mrs. Hess were clients of his firm from September 1997 until September of 2000. We discovered this at the arbitration.

Start-up Company in Seattle/Bellevue

On June 15, 2001 the Company PFP plan administrators was formed by Mr. Paleveda, Glenn Price and Charles Farrington and Bill Faiferlick a local insurance agent. Stock was issued in the following amount 37.5% to Nick Paleveda, 37.5% to Bill Faiferlick and 25% to Price and Farrington. In addition, 50% of the stock was held as Treasury stock. Mr. Paleveda was elected President and CEO of the Company and held this office since the beginning of the company. The company PFP plan administrators also filed a d/b/a as The 412(i)Company. The company administers 412(i) defined benefit plans for insurance companies through the internet.

On or about October 1, 2003 Paul R. Hess J.D. was retained to assist the reorganization of the company. Paul Hess had known Nick Paleveda the CEO of the company for 3 years. Mrs. Jan Hess told Mr. Paleveda that Mr. Paul Hess was an attorney and a member of the Kansas Bar. Ms. Hess stated she was married to Mr. Hess and Mr. Hess stated that indeed they were married. Mr. Hess also made the statement he was an attorney and member of the Kansas Bar and produced a biography that stated he was married to Jan Hess and a Kansas Attorney. (Mr. Hess was in fact not married, discovered at the arbitration and a disbarred attorney this evidence was presented to Mr. Easter and he ignored it- because he had a hidden relationship with the defendant.)

On or about November 1, 2002, the company was reorganized giving Mr. Paleveda 82.5% of the stock, Price and Farrington 12.5% of the stock and Mr. Hess 2.5% of the stock. Mr. Farrington held the corporate insurance license as he was also an insurance agent. Mr. Hess was invited to join the company as a part time consultant on November 1, 2003. Mr. Hess claimed that he had been the COO for many other companies and as an attorney would be available for full time COO position at the 412(i)Company starting in January of 2003.

On or about February 1, 2003 Mr. Paleveda asked Mr. Hess to become the COO of the company and a full time employee. Mr. Hess received a salary of $85,000 per year and the salaries were administered through Paychecks.

On March 7, 2003 Mr. Hess approached Mr. Paleveda about a bonus structure. He said we needed to give the employees an incentive to continue working at the company. Mr. Paleveda listened and Mr. Hess suggested .05% for Sharon Angel, .05% for Doug Farrar, 2.5% for Erik Shaner and 8% for Mr. Hess. He explained the bonuses would be non-binding. Mr. Paleveda stated that the bonus structure needed to be non-binding as the company was a start-up company. Mr. Hess assured him that would be the case. Mr. Hess presented a written contract for himself at 8% which Mr. Paleveda refused to sign as the bonus (if any) could only be paid after the solvency of the company was assured. Mr. Paleveda informed Mr. Hess he would need an insurance license to receive bonuses. Mr. Hess said he would get a license. Mr. Paleveda never signed the agreement and Mr. Hess never obtained his insurance license. On or about

March 11, 2003 Mr. Hess presented another contract to Mr. Paleveda regarding his own compensation package. Mr. Paleveda disagreed with the arrangement due to the start up nature of the company and did not enter into a contract. Mr. Hess continued working for the $85,000 salary.

In July of 2003, Mr. Hess then realized that a check in the amount of $146,181.90 was coming to the company. Mr. Hess wanted to quit the company as the office was moved from Bellevue to Bellingham Washington. Mr. Hess then devised a scheme to open a secret bank account in Bellevue under the name PFP Plan administrators. Mr. Hess then diverted the check that was written to PFP Plan Administrators from Bellingham to Bellevue into the secret bank account as the check was written to the company and into his personal bank account. This was all done without the knowledge and consent of Mr. Paleveda, the CEO and majority shareholder.

Mr. Price and Mr. Farrington were promised funds from this check by Mr. Hess and Mr. Farrington was asked to revoke the corporate license without anyone's knowledge and to take the funds into his own name. Mr. Price and Farrington's practice was in bad financial shape and the golden opportunity to receive significant money came to them. Mr. Price and Mr. Farrington did not know at this time Mr. Hess was a convicted felon and disbarred attorney. Mr. Hess went to 2 of the board members Charles Farrington, and Glenn Price and convinced them they would not get paid well unless the money was seized and cashier's checks written to them. Mr. Price and Mr. Farrington then convened a board meeting and did not invite Mr. Paleveda. (This is clearly against Washington State law and ignored by Mr. Easter who protected his client at the arbitration.) He also convinced Mr. Farrington that he could sign his name to two cases, the Minas case and the Ludeman case and receive commissions in the amount of $35,000 and $117,000 respectfully.

Mr. Hess then made up statements to Mr. Price and Mr. Farrington that the company was not being run correctly and Mr. Paleveda and Ms. Ewing were bad people. Mr. Price and Mr. Farrington did not work in the company, spent no time working at the company but were desperate for money. (In June, Mr. Price had complained to Mr. Paleveda that Price and Farrington were in the worse financial position in 10 years.)

With no knowledge given to Mr. Paleveda, Mr. Hess Price and Farrington held a secret board meeting, did not invite Mr. Paleveda and made a statement that he was not invited. (This was admitted into evidence and ignored by Mr. Easter. Under Washington law it is clear that board members need to be notified for a special meeting see RCW 48.17.490.)

The defendants held an illegal board meeting between the two of them to approve of the embezzlement and did not notify Mr. Paleveda. The embezzlement took place in secrecy until all the cashier's checks were issued to themselves-then then notified Mr. Paleveda. They told Mr. Paleveda that we notified you so we would not be arrested for embezzlement- as attorneys they knew the law and that in Washington they would not be arrested. Mr. Price said as a former prosecutor he said "knew that the police would do nothing. "

Mr. Farrington also revoked the corporate licenses and placed himself as agent of record on all the cases. Mr. Farrington then took a $35,000.00 commission personally that was due to the company. On July 18th 2003 Mr. Hess, Mr. Farrington, and Mr. Price seized the check that was written to The 412(i)Company in the amount of $146,181.90. This check was written to the company intended for payroll. Mr. Hess, Farrington and Price knew this and wanted to embezzle the funds for their own use. In order to accomplish this goal they opened up a separate bank account without the knowledge consent or approval of the

Board member, majority shareholder, CEO and President Nick Paleveda. They secretly deposited the check in the new bank account on 7/24/03 and secretly issued cashier's checks to themselves on 8/01/03 once they accomplished their embezzlement goals, they notified Mr. Paleveda on 8/8/03.

Mr. Hess, Price, and Farrington new bank account was only used for the embezzlement. They deposited the funds in the bank account and wrote cashier's checks to themselves in the amount of $77,608.00 to Mr. Hess $19,285 to Mr. Shaner, $13,336 to Mr. Price and Mr. Farrington and $3,626 to Mr. Farrar, and $1,774 to Mrs. Angel. Mr. Price, Farrington and Hess then all resigned from the company and tendered back their stock. Mr. Paleveda, the CEO of the company, Board member and 82.5% shareholder was unaware of all this until an e-mail was sent August 9th explaining what they did.

Mr. Hess claimed, after the funds were embezzled, that the company was not being run properly and that he may not get his bonus so he embezzled it. Mr. Price and Mr. Farrington, whose law firm practice was in the worst financial shape in 10 years, made a deal with Mr. Hess to take $35,000 as the commission for a case they had no involvement and an additional $13,336.00 with the hope to take another commission of $117,000.00 to give them a grand total of $134,880.00. Mr. Hess showed Mr. Farrington how he could change the name on cases he never worked on from the company to his individual name and pocket a quick $35,000.00.

The following Monday August 11th, Mr. Paleveda then contacted the Bellevue Police department. The police informed Mr. Paleveda that Mr. Hess was not an attorney and was in fact disbarred in 1986. Mr. Hess was charged in 1985 with two counts of felony theft in Kansas and pleaded guilty to one count of felony theft. Mr. Paleveda was totally unaware of Mr. Hess having a criminal record or disbarment. Mr. Paleveda was always under the understanding that Mr. Hess was a member in good standing of the Kansas Bar and did not know about the convictions. Mr. Paleveda discovered that Mr. Hess had arrest and convictions in 1986, 1987, 1992 and 1994 including theft, forgery, securities fraud, trafficking in illegal goods and taxes. Mr. Paleveda was totally unaware of his past convictions and shocked and dismayed not only about the embezzlement but the disbarment as well.

When the police arrived at the door of Price and Farrington. (Mr. Price, who was also involved in the embezzlement would not allow the police in the office it was also at this time Mr. Price and Farrington became aware of Hess' convictions.) Mr. Paleveda showed up later and asked for the funds back and received part of the funds back in the amount of $29,689.90. Mr. Paleveda then went to Mr. Shaner and he returned part of the funds as well. Mr. Paleveda approached Ms. Angel and she returns all the funds.

Mr. Hess refuses to return the funds, has threatened to turn the corporation over to the IRS if anything was made of the embezzlement. These threats were in writing and entered into evidence and ignored by Mr. Easter in his "reasoned opinion". Mr. Price and Farrington also refused to return all of the embezzled funds as well as Mr. Farrar who stated he had a "deal" with Mr. Hess and was going to keep the embezzled funds.

Mr. Paleveda filed a Bar complaint against Mr. Price and Mr. Farrington who defended saying "it was their fiduciary duty" to take the funds and give them to Mr. Hess Mr. Price and Farrington. Mr. Price produced an unsigned document to support Mr. Hess. When Mr. Paleveda said the document was a forgery and unsigned Mr. Farrington replied "it doesn't matter we want the money." When Mr. Paleveda demanded the funds be returned to the company as the check was a corporate check Mr. Price got angry and upset and pounded on the table with his fist at which time Mr. Paleveda left and filed a complaint to the Bar, and a civil action. The Bar complaint has been stayed pending the outcome of this matter.

The Superior Court of Whatcom County ordered the case to Arbitration even though the case fell outside the "Licensing and Technology Agreement" which did not cover corporate disputes or insurance contract law.

They needed additional information

MARCH, 2006

Felicia P. Congalton
Senior Disciplinary Counsel
Washington State Bar Association
2102 Fourth Ave. #400 Seattle Washington 98121-2330

Re: WSBA File: 06-01408
   Scott Easter "Montgomery Purdue"
   RE: BANK FRAUD /Money Laundering

Dear Ms. Congalton,

Please find attached part of the evidence that Mr. Easter conveniently forgot to mention that was part of the arbitration. You will find attached a Bank application made out by one of Mr. Hess's associates, a Washington Bar member named Charles Farrington. (Who I also have a pending complaint). This is the bank application made out to embezzle the $146,000.00 check from the412iCompany. One of the 412iCompany employees pointed out that the entire application was fraudulent except for Mr. Farrington's signature.

Please note the following Bank Fraud:

1. Gross sales states; $30,000.00 during that point in time the company had grossed nearly $100,000.00 and Mr. Farrington was depositing a check of over $146,000.00-Obvious BANK FRAUD.

2. Number of Employees: 1. At the time of the application there were 8 full time employees. When Mr. Farrington issued cashier's checks to himself and other employees he knew that more than one employee worked at the company-see master application-Obvious BANK FRAUD.

3. Number of Locations 1. The 412iCompany had 2 locations, one in Bellevue and one in Bellingham. Mr. Farrington knew that there were two locations and he placed 1-Obvious BANK FRAUD.

4. Information about Key Employees: Mr. Farrington listed only one employee-himself-and he was not even an employee. The key employee at that time was Nick Paleveda-me, the CEO and 80% shareholder-Obvious BANK FRAUD.

THE FINAL STEP WAS CASHIER'S CHECKS totaling nearly $146,000.00 WERE WRITTEN FROM THIS ACCOUNT TO MR. HESS, PRICE AND FARRINGTON, and SHANER-and to a lesser extent others.

ALL this evidence (and more) was introduced to Mr. Easter at the arbitration. He chose to ignore the evidence and granted the defendant's nearly $100,000 in attorney's fees-WHY?
These are our theories

1. His firm had a "hidden relationship" with Paul Hess, the defendant in this case and

professional white collar criminal. This was discovered at the arbitration.

2. He wanted repeat business from Mr. Zimbleman as he was chosen by Mr. Zimbleman in the past for arbitration.

3. He did not want to "offend" his fellow Bar members Mr. Price and Mr. Farrington and upset the "Seattle legal community".

4. He was "paid to do a job"-many former employees of The412iCompany believe he received some sort of payment-The record reflects he was paid in the past by Hess above the table.

5. Another theory is he may have received under the table payments. I have no proof at this time regarding this theory, although Hess has made "cash payments" to other parties in the past. However, Mr. Easter hiding his relationship with Mr. Hess, and creating a "reasoned opinion" that did not follow the facts of the case or law in the state of Washington certainly has given credence to this theory.

Whatever theory, whatever "Latin phrase" that may be used-nothing can defend the actions taken by Hess, Farrington and associates.

And they needed even more information.

October 20, 2006

Felice P. Congalton
Senior Disciplinary Counsel
Washington State Bar Association
1325 4th Avenue Suite 600
Seattle WA. 98101-2539

Re: WSBA File: 06-01408

Scott Easter "Montgomery Purdue"

RE: BANK FRAUD /Money Laundering

Dear Ms. Congalton,

This letter is to inform you of our continuing investigation of Mr. Hess, Mr. Easter, Mr. Price and Mr. Farrington. It appears from our investigation that Mr. Price and Mr. Farrington, members of the Washington Bar Association conspired with Mr. Hess a disbarred convicted felon, to embezzle and did embezzle $146,000.00 from a company, (now in bankruptcy) known as The412(i)Company. When the lawsuit against these men Hess, Price, and Farrington appeared before Mr. Scott Easter, of Montgomery Purdue, Mr. Easter refused to disclose his firm's Montgomery Purdue's relationship with Mr. Hess.

In fact his firm held title to Mr. Hess's house for 3 years and we believe collected substantial fees or other monetary gain from Hess. Mr. Easter awarded nearly $100,000.00 to the Hess trio and ignored Washington law in the process. I am a member of the Florida Bar and a witness to this corruption. I have asked the Washington Bar Association to investigate this matter and have not received an adequate response. Is this "business as usual" in the State of Washington. I would like to know the status of the investigation- is there an investigation? To date I have seen no action by the Washington Bar.

The Insurance Commissioner of the State of Washington has investigated and recently reprimanded Mr. Farrington for violating Washington law-(splitting insurance commissions with a non-licensed agent-Hess and Price). I am grateful for the Insurance Commissioner to stand up and investigate this matter and issue the reprimand.

Mr. Easter who appears to be the Hess family attorney awarded Mr. Hess's group nearly $100,000.00 and nothing has happened to him. Mr. Farrington and Mr. Price, who I have complaints against before the Washington Bar-Nothing has happened to them.

Nick Paleveda MBA J.D. LL.M
CEO Executive Benefits Design Group

He had no problem in violating all of these to give his buddy Eric Zimbelman a nice award and keep his other buddy/client Paul Hess out of trouble. Little did he know that we knew his firm had a relationship with the defendant, and little did we know of the massive extent of the relationship? Actually, to this day we really don't know. All we have is 324 pages of correspondence that we received by way of a federal subpoena to their firm.

In most cases it is illegal or unethical to lie before a federal judge or officer, but this is not the cases with attorneys who practice before arbitrators, at least that were the ruling by the Washington State Bar Association.

Generally Bar Associations are strict in following ethical rules such as Florida where I am licensed to practice. It is "unethical" to run an advertisement without approval from the Bar. You can be disbarred for not returning a client's phone call. You can be disbarred for not staying in communication with your client etc.

In Washington, the rules are different. There are no rules...... on advertising, there are no rules...... about lying which are enforced, and there are no rules..... about creating fake bank accounts. What comfort it is to live and work in the wild-wild west. No wonder O.J. ordered up a "posse" in Las Vegas to get his stuff back. No wonder he was not prosecuted for murder with DNA all over the victim's body. The only good of the trial is it demonstrated to the USA the legal system ineptness in certain parts of the West The good news is most con-men do not come to Washington, they go to Florida (where I am from) and the system recognizes them and prosecutes them. In Washington, the Kansas con-men have a field day as the system does not exist to handle the few con-men in the state.

Chapter 16

"Pattern of behavior"

Q-Pharma was the company Paul Hess had worked for prior to setting up shop at The 412(i)Company. When I contacted Joe Baba, the former CEO of Q-Pharma, he informed me of the same sad story with Paul Hess. "Yes", said Joe, Paul introduced himself as an attorney from Kansas. "Once he came to the company, all hell broke loose." He said, "Paul divided the loyalties between the employees eventually we ended up in court".

Joe felt that Q-Pharma would have worked out well if it was not for the Hess family which sent Q-Pharma to an early grave. Next I contacted Ari Cowan from EDVITA, a company Paul had worked for prior to Q-Pharma.

"Come to Bellevue, and I will talk to you" said Ari. "I don't want to discuss this over the phone." EDVITA was still in operation.

I, Warren Wheeler , solemnly declare as follows:

1. I am Warren Wheeler, former member of the Board of Directors of Seminar Master and I know Paul R. Hess personally.

2. I am over the age of eighteen years and make this declaration on personal knowledge.

3. I was on the Board of Directors of Seminar Master when I met Paul Hess who stated he was an attorney. Seminar Masters was in need of legal help so he was hired as General Counsel of the corporation. We understood he was a member of the Kansas Bar and had served in the Kansas Legislature.

4. When Mr. Hess was hired the company ran into turmoil due to his lies and deception with the employees and

management of Seminar Masters. He had secret meetings with the financial backers of the company and secret meetings with Board members. These meetings created fractions within the organization.

5. On one occasion, an ophthalmologist met with Paul Hess to invest in the company Seminar Masters. Mr. Hess diverted the investment funds into his own Jewelry business. Mr. Hess gave the investor a 2d mortgage for the investment which was on his house in Shoreline, which later was discovered to have multiple second mortgages.

6. When the investor wanted her money back, she threatened to sue Seminar Masters as Mr. Hess obtained the loan on company time. The board then hired an attorney in Seattle to investigate Mr. Hess. The attorney discovered that Mr. Hess was not an attorney and he was fired.

7. Mr. Hess created such discontent that many employees also left the

company. Once Mr. Hess was fired he went back that evening and took corporate files creating many missing important files at the company. I recently discovered he is not married to Jan Hess.

8. Mr. Hess and his "partner" were successful in contributing to the destruction of Seminar Masters.

Once Preston Gates good and honest and ethical attorney Paul Lawrence lost our motion against the not as good but ethically challenged attorney Erik Zimbelman, before an elected state judge who had been on the bench for less than 6 months, the company was major league insolvent. I give Paul Lawrence credit for coming to Bellingham. Most attorneys will not travel to Bellingham because the reputation of the legal community in Bellingham is it is backwards. Most Bellingham lawyers will not go to Seattle because they think it is corrupt. The judge...Snyder...did not want to overturn the arbitrator, thinking that a "little conflict" would not affect the award-do not mention the manifest disregard for the law as the arbitrator has "discretion over law and fact" (even if he is ethically challenged like Scott Easter". The blame of the failure of The412(i)Company is with Scott Easter. Here he had an opportunity to correct a wrong; however he was preoccupied by his relationship with Hess and Zimbleman. He is "untouchable" as he is the sole decider of law and fact and is "immune" from legal process. There is no way to write the wrongs of Scott Easter. Protected by the Bar and the American Arbitration Association, he waits for his next client or victim in the tallest building in Seattle.

Chapter 17

BANKRUPTCY

Time for plan "B". Company has no money to pay legal fees for them, legal fees for us and "bonus" money for them. Let's go to Federal Court.....or Bankruptcy. These courts are courts of last resort where the legal system in some cases really did not work, which happened to be our case. In the meantime, Zimbelman started issuing writs of attachments on our accounts and seized the profit sharing plan! Now everyone knows law 101, he cannot garnish the pension-but out west, this is not true. The fact is the profit sharing plan is protected under ERISA in all parts of the U.S.-but...not Washington State. When we asked him to return the funds – or help-he refused. In the meantime Key Bank kept hold of the funds. When we asked Key Bank to put the funds back in the plan-they refused. The trustee did not help either. Wait-those are employee ERISA funds- it is against the law! They are protected from creditors. Well, this is Washington!

The Law Firm of Lester and Hydal sits next to the Courthouse in Whatcom County. Tome Lester was retained to bring back the pension funds. Tom had attended law school in Iowa and had made Bellingham his home. Well versed in the procedure to have the pension funds returned he filed a motion to bring back the funds to the plan. "Who is your trustee?" he asked> Peter Arkison we said. "Oh no!" he said, "he takes bribes". This was just what we wanted to hear. No hearing date was set as the pension funds and the case proceeded to Federal Court.

The Department of Labor was contacted about the diversion of funds, but frankly it was too small, only amounting to several thousand dollars.

Peter Arkison's office sits in the basement of the key bank Building in downtown Bellingham. A small frail elderly gentleman, he had been in the community since the dawn of man. Most of his days are spent wringing out funds from wiped out bankruptcy victims to line the coffers of the bankruptcy estate which he delightfully shares in the proceeds.

The Bankruptcy proceedings did not start out well. Denise Mowes who represented the trustee Pater Arkison, made her first move on the motion calendar which was to "abandon" the appeal that Preston Gates had outlined. Peter Arkison wanted to "throw out" the largest asset of the estate! Denise shows up to court in a mini-skirt, which happens to be her "trademark style". Never a smile on her face, a serious and somber mood is projected for all to see and feel. We fought the trustee's abandonment of the appeal, but with the 'weight of the trustee" firmly letting Hess off the hook, we lost the dismissal. Next,

144

the trustee made a "surprising move". Rather than trying to obtain the funds left in the account for the corporation, they made a motion to abandon the funds in favor of 'the Hess group". We fought that- hard! Why didn't the trustee ask for these funds to be part of the estate? Maybe the statement "he takes bribes" has merit. The trustee also sent a letter stating that he "found money" to the court. What does that mean? He also sent a letter to the court stating he wanted to enter into a "Hess Compromise". Now we know Arkison was holding "secret meetings with Hess"- Great!

The day finally arrived to determine the ownership of the Lafayette overrides which has now totaled over $70,000.00 The trustee's attorney Denise Mowes filed a motion to "abandon the funds" to Farrington as the trustee could not figure they had any ownership rights as the 1099 was issued jointly to Farrington and The412(i)Company. "What?" "Give $70,000 to Farrington!" I said, "He is the one who committed bank fraud to bring down the company and now the trustee wants to give him $70,000.00!" We went through the records and the records showed the contract was issued to PFP with Farrington as the corporate agent. There was also another contract with Farrington as an individual but is unsigned by Lafayette.

Eric Zimbleman and Charles Farrington arrived in Federal Court. They were both well dressed and smug waiting for a big payday. Farrington knew he did not work on any of the cases and was not entitled to any of the overrides from the policies, but the thought of making a quick $70,000.00 or more was too much to give up. Not only that, they had spent a lot of time and money in legal fees to maintain the booty taken by the secret bank account. Why not try for more. The paperwork is confusing. Farrington had signed the corporate papers as an individual and as an officer of the company-both! Now his attorney could argue in this case, the money should be awarded to him as an individual and bypass the company.

Andrew Guy at Stole Rives just wanted Lafayette out of this contest. Lafayette Life was holding the overrides for the winner of this battle but did not want to be sued by the loser. In careful corporate format, Andy Guy had papers drawn up by all parties exonerating his client from future liability.

Charles Farrington continued to battle for the overrides claiming they were all his. In December of 2007, just before Christmas, the trustee sought to give Charles Farrington a Christmas gift of about $70,000.00-all the Lafayette corporate overrides and funds. Our attorneys objected to this demonstrating that Farrington was not entitled to these funds as they belonged to the corporation. In fact Farrington had done nothing to earn these funds. It was not a surprise to see Farrington attempt to exert ownership over the corporate funds, but it now made sense why the contracts signed by Farrington were handled so poorly. Farrington was attempting as early as May of 2003 to route the funds into his own personal account. He was frustrated as all the funds kept coming to the company. Hess showed up at the right time and helped him create the "secret" bank account which Farrington used to route the corporate funds into his personal account. In every other state it is called "money laundering". In Washington, with the assistance of Scott Easter, it was just another day in the Emerald city.

An issue never decided in the arbitration was the company management overrides and commissions. The412iCompany had a contract with Lafayette Life to be paid overrides from Lafayette. Farrington had licensed the company to receive the funds in accordance with State Law. Farrington was now claiming all the funds were his personally. Upon reviewing the files, we noticed that all the checks regarding these contracts came out in PFP Plan Administrators, the 412(i) Company name, not in Farrington's name. This is probably what provoked the "secret bank account "in August of 2002. Farrington was frustrated that the checks were being issued in the company name-not in his. He could not legally embezzle the funds, so he opened up a bank account in the corporate name- and routed the funds to his new friend Paul Hess and himself and Glenn Price. In a public company situation, he would be indicted for this action. In Washington State, with a private company, indictment was beyond question. The contracts were signed with PFP Plan administrators/The 412(i)Company but he marked the box "individual". In most states, including Washington, there is a "duty of loyalty" to the company-but that is law 101. There exist the "corporate opportunity doctrine" as well-you cannot just take corporate assets and claim them as your own-or can you?

Finally the day of the hearing arrived. Charles Farrington was claiming over $70,000 of funds which he did not earn and held no involvement. We were confident the law was on our side, the facts were on our side, but the trustee was not. The trustee in theory, represent the creditors, but that is law 101. Law 102, is the trustee does what the trustee wants with no regard for the law. I talked to the attorney for ARIS, Don Bailey an AV rated attorney and he was confident in our chances.

Good Friday 2008 came early on March 24, 2008, This event occurs once every approximately 400 years as Easter must land on the Sunday following a full moon after the spring equinox, and the decision of the court came with it-ordering all the funds to Farrington. The trial court disregarded the facts and the law, however looked at the trustee motioning all the funds to Farrington. This is quite odd, but this is Washington and we have become familiar with the problems of the wild west. With the "weight of the trustee" behind Farrington-we lost the funds to Farrington. Now all there is to do is to appeal the decision, lest Farrington, the originator of secret bank accounts, committing bank fraud is now rewarded with $70,000.00

The final chapter cannot end this way. Charles Farrington riding off into the sunset with baskets of money after he initiated an embezzlement with Paul Hess. Only one thing left, and that is to appeal the decision. In Washington, there is apathy when it comes to white collar crime especially among Washington lawyers. In contacting lawyers about this issue, they are annoyed that anyone would even challenge "the system".

Unfortunately for them we plan an appeal to the BAP of the 9th Circuit. I was excited to learn that no judges from Washington sat on the BAP. This is good news! Perhaps a good intelligent person will actually show up and look at this case for what it is and what it stands for.

The appellate process-We lost!!!- another $72,000 down the drain plus $145,000=$217,000 in total funds diverted. Of course this is an "unpublished opinion" as the judges could not follow the law and allow Farrington to receive $72,000 at the same time. What they do not teach you in law school is they can just "make it up" or "ignore it". The reason is quite simple, the BK Judge relied on the trustee and the BAP relies on the BK judge and the 9th Circuit relies on the BAP. The trustee "found money" and diverted the funds to Farrington. The trustee has "quasi judicial immunity" and since this was approved by the Court, can rest now in comfort. In the meantime Hess rest in comfort in his Million Dollar Home, Price in an $800,000 home and Farrington in his new home on the Sammamish Plateau. Who said crime doesn't pay?

Next, the trustee turned on us. Arksion sued the administration company claiming it was a "successor corporation".
What is not taught in law school is judges come in all shapes and sizes. They are people with moods and in some cases not sensible. In the main case, the trustee had filed for a summary judgment against the administration company for transfers. The judge dismissed the motion. We were not sure about this, however the political climate favored us—for the first time. Political climate-they do not teach you that in law school. Our administration company was represented by Mr. Bailey a well respected Seattle attorney-who actually has ethics. The politics of a courtroom- who knows who can be as important as the law and the facts.

Fortunately, ARIS had Don Bailey, a well known attorney in the court representing ARIS and Arksion's complaint was dismissed...but that did not stop hi,

Arkison did a search and replace- why not make the same allegations against Executive Benefits? I had formed a company after the bankruptcy and needed a place to go to work. The employee's needed jobs so I hired them. These people should not lose their job because some jerk lawyers steal money. In Arksion's complaint he used the affidavit from their expert that A.R.I.S. was the successor and received the transfers-but filed against Executive Benefits anyway. Who cares about the facts? Who cares about the law? This is Washington! Unfortunately, the political climate was against us as the attorney had not appeared many, many times before Glover, so he lashed out..."Paleveda, I don't believe anything Paleveda says". Now this is unfortunate because the Judge had no knowledge of anything that was said that was untrue. He ruled of course in favor of Peter Arkison-now the 412(i)Company Successor is....Executive Benefits! In addition, the company owes the trustee $300,000.00!

Facts-who cares the affidavit from the expert is against A.R.I.S.-not Executive Benefits. Who cares there are not the same shareholders-in fact no common shareholders. Who cares they are not the same companies. Who cares they are not the same business. Who cares the company was formed well after 412(i) Company went insolvent. None of this mattered to Glover- all he was looking for was asserting his power over the court and his soon to be retirement. Now he was powerful, perhaps his reason to be a judge- drunk with power. No concern for the truth, no concern for the law. Judges, however have very little accountability and hence are free to do as they please within limits only by the courts. Most judges are good and honest people. However if you get a bad trustee, with a crooked arbitrator and poor judge, no matter what the law is ....no matter what the facts are... the result can be disastrous. Removing a federal judge would be like moving an iceberg from the middle of the Atlantic ocean, not impossible but close to it. Some law firms have total disregard for the ethics (as we saw) in any situation. It is about greed, money and power. Many people attracted to law school attend based on these principles. GMP,-Greed, Money and Power, not GNP is the driving force for many attorneys. This can dictate the outcome of our lives if not controlled. We go back to work. We prepare to file an appeal and a motion to recuse himself. A recusal motion is interesting. The judge who is hearing your case must accept or deny the recusal. I filed the motion, and Arkison ask for sanctions. Now this is totally against procedure, but he argued anyway-through his counsel-he generally is like most bullies, never shows his own face.

Jim Sturdevant, the attorney for Peter Pearce called and said.

"All good except under Bankruptcy rule 5004 it is actually under section 455(a) not 144." Of course anything Jim does, he has to be careful not to make waves as he has other clients in the BK courts.

The day of the motion to recuse is set. Nothing in the law is simple. The person who grants the motion has to be Glover himself. Glover calls first thing on the calendar, this motion. He states" I don't want this thing to get out of hand-I am denying the motion and denying the opponents motion for sanctions." And the case moves on. We knew the standards are quite high to show bias-but how can a judge who doesn't believe anything one party says have anything but bias. Would any reasonable person walk into any reasonable courtroom with a judge who doesn't believe a word of the other party?

Funny, what they tell you in law school is you need to examine the facts, and apply the law. In Washington, you need to examine "The Political situation" then look at the facts and law. In some cases, ignore the law look at the political situation-who knows who and who has what bias. The value of a legal education is questionable if decisions are made like this, and they are done so at an alarming rate. The cost of a legal education continues to rise. Today, my law school education for tuition alone would be $140,000. Ouch! In law school you become indoctrinated about judicial fairness and ethics. After you graduate, you believe in the system. Then you work in the system and get exposed to petite corruption, major corruption and interest in pecuniary gain exceeding justice. After about 10 years in practice, you realize that the judicial education was a false utopia-oops.

The students who received jobs at large law firms had the right connections or were incredible workaholics. The balance went to work for the government and the rest joined the unemployment lines. Everyone in law school likes attorneys and everyone who did not hates attorneys. The profession gives them reasons for both points of view. There are of course the good attorneys and honest ones, and there are the dogs which cannot be removed – many become litigators.

Chapter 18

**IN THE 9TH CIRCUIT COURT OF
APPEALS**
"The Battle in Seattle continues"...

The Ninth Circuit Court of Appeals is the last stop before the Supreme Court of the United States. The Ninth Circuit is located in San Francisco California and is the largest of the appellate courts in the U.S. spanning the entire west and Alaska and Hawaii. The Ninth Circuit also has an office in Seattle where the "battle of Seattle continued to take place. The "Hess Group" somehow purchased the favor of the trustee who not only dismissed the appeal allowing the arbitrator to maintain a conflict of interest but also sued Executive Benefits as a "successor corporation" and for "fraudulent conveyance". The trustee went to his favorite judge who he had a relationship with for more than thirty years and received a favorable judgment of over $300,000.00. The problem is that the trustee's own expert pointed out that "A.R.I.S." was the successor corporation not "Executive Benefits". The judge chose to overlook the expert report from the trustee and ruled in favor of the trustee anyway.

What can you do? APPEAL! We appealed the case now to the Western District of Washington where the judge quickly upheld the decision of the bankruptcy court. The decision was a "summary judgment" which in layman's term is that you do not get a trial.-frankly we have NEVER had a trial in this 10 year battle. The judge ruled as a "matter of law" you are guilty. We then appealed to the 9th Circuit Court of Appeals. Just as the appeal was taking place, the U.S. Supreme Court ruled in *Stern v. Marshall* that Bankruptcy Courts cannot hear claims like fraudulent conveyance where the defendant never filed a proof of claim before the court. This, according to the Supreme Court of the United States, is because of the "inadequate protections" in bankruptcy court by Article I judges-oh really! I just had first hand experience with that concept. In our case, we never filed a claim for Executive Benefits as it had nothing to do with The412(i)Company. We asked the court that this crazy $300,000 judgment be vacated. The Supreme Court went on in their decision that bankruptcy courts do not afford the same protection as a state court or federal court-in English you do not get a trial by jury. Hence- they should not be able to listen to these types of cases.

Outsiders can dispute the logic of this decision by the Supreme Court, however when bankruptcy Courts operate like Bankruptcy Clubs, there is no doubt in my mind you do not want an outside issue heard by this court.

The Chief Judge of the Ninth Circuit also was chosen to hear this case. I was on a high! To actually be able to argue before the 9th Circuit Court of Appeals! Questions flared from the bench." How come you did not bring up *Stern v. Marshall* in your opening brief" said Chief Judge Kolzinski? "Well, it had not been decided until after the opening brief was filed, hence I put it into my reply brief" I said. The Chief Judge was satisfied with the answer. "Wasn't the Marshall case about defamation" he asked. "No it was about fraudulent conveyance." I said. Then I remembered, "Your honor, the case was a defamation case, but the opinion spoke at length about not allowing fraudulent conveyance cases to be heard before bankruptcy courts". This occurred where no claims were filed with the bankruptcy courts as in another Supreme Court case called "*Grandfinanceria*".

Next, the attorney for the trustee spoke. "Can you give me the cases in your support?" –said the judge? "Well, I just looked at them last week" she replied. The judges were outraged. How can you come to court and not be prepared. They hammered her with grueling questions that she could not answer and even had me feeling sorry for her. When we left the courtroom we took the same elevator. A friend of mine Ron Johnson had driven down with me from Bellingham. "Well, I guess you will have time to make it to your baseball game I said to my friend." Then we all exited from the elevator.

Chapter 19.

THE NINTH CIRCUIT LOOKS FOR A FRIEND-AMICUS CURAIE

We were hoping to finally receive a favorable decision in this mess when the Ninth Circuit asked for an "amicus brief" which means a "friend of the court" or an outside opinion relating to whether fraudulent conveyance issues can be heard by a bankruptcy judge. I quickly looked on the internet and found AOTA and the National Black Chamber of Commerce who had filed "amicus briefs" in the *Stern v. Marshall* case and contacted them. Our little case now had National importance as bankruptcy trustees were chasing victims of the Madoff scandal in New York under the guise of "fraudulent conveyance." In addition, if we won nearly 1.6 million cases in bankruptcy court may get transferred to Federal or State courts. However can you imagine that you just became a victim of a fraud and now the Bankruptcy trustee wants you to return funds you do not have and can do this without a trial? You now become another victim of the Bankruptcy club.

Chapter 19

THE DEPARTMENT OF JUSTICE

If you haven't noticed already, when something goes wrong in your life the Federal Government arrives just in the nick of time... and then takes the other side. When Mutual Benefit failed, which is today the largest failure of any life insurance company, the government stepped in to take over all the assets and then.... went after all the agents of the company who had just lost their jobs. In this case the DOJ now intervenes citing that the case is of great public interest as they do not want "their bankruptcy trustees" to have to fight in court with a jury for the "fraudulent conveyance" claims. It is much easier for a bankruptcy trustee to claim "foul" have the claim rubber stamped by a BK judge and let the defendant not have jury trial.

Unfortunately for the DOJ, the Supreme Court did not see it this way. The Supreme Court actually believes in the jury system albeit a 5-4 decision. Frankly, the DOJ is on the wrong side of this issue. If the U.S. keeps creating justice by eliminating juries, we will have evolved into a 3d world judicial system. In English, unless you are a lawyer or a judge, you have no voice in the judicial process. The DOJ's prior argument is that it will cost money to have a jury listen to a claim. They are correct... tyranny and dictatorships are less expensive and time consuming to manage then democracy-and jury trials...and your point is?????

Chapter 20

AMICUS BRIEFS

The Ninth Circuit requested Amicus briefs known as "friends of the court" to determine the issue whether a bankruptcy judge can listen to a claim brought by a bankruptcy trustee involving a non-creditor of the estate. Stern appeared to rule that the non-creditor could ask and request and receive a jury trial, not a trial by "summary judgment". At first I thought no amicus briefs would be filed except by the Department of Justice which filed a motion to allow time to file a brief. The Department of Justice of the United States (the same department that withheld information form Ted Stevens case which would have exonerated him) really did not want their bankruptcy trustees to have to go to a real court outside of bankruptcy and have to litigate claims where it is

simple for them to ask for a summary
judgment from the bankruptcy judge and
have the summary judgment upheld by
the higher courts a/k/a rubber stamp
justice. The jury? Who needs them!
Summary judgment is designed to do
away with the jury system of the United
States and allow the bankruptcy trustee to
be judge, jury and executioner.

In any event the amicus briefs started to
roll in. First from attorney's who had
clients like mine who were screwed in the
bankruptcy court-obviously these briefs
were in my favor. Next from law professors
who thought Bankruptcy judges should
have this "great power" over non parties
and allow them to slam non-parties at will.
Obviously these briefs were against us.
Finally "big law" stepped in. These are
some of the largest law firms in the United
States which charge $500 an hour up for
their time. These briefs were actually in
my favor! Jones Day, the 3d largest law
firm in the U.S. and Ropes and Gray one

of the top 20 law firms in the U.S. wrote briefs in my favor. During this time the 7th circuit also wrote a brief and decided a case in my favor In Re Ortiz. You have got to like the 7th Circuit. This Circuit I follow a lot as they take on complex pension cases and was the first circuit to rule in a Floor-Offset case.

What will the 9th Circuit do? Will they follow the 7th? Will they carve out an exception in favor of the trustee? What about the expert witness report that the trustee paid for that says "A.R.I.S" is the successor trustee-why did all the briefs ignore this report? Why does the trustee ignore this report? Why does the bankruptcy judge ignore this report? Come on this is a SUMMARY JUDGMENT! Can the judge throw the expert witness report paid for by the trustee who is adverse to the trustee under the bus and ram a summary judgment down my throat? Do we ever get our day in court before an "independent" jury? The briefs of

"the amicus" that are against us argued
we "waived our right to a jury" in that we
did not file a "motion to withdraw the
reference". But it is not true. I checked
and our attorney stated quite clearly that
he wanted a jury trial and that this case is
not to be heard by the bankruptcy court.
There was no "waiver", not even close.
After filing this and sending the case to
the District court for a trial, the trustee
filed for a summary judgment and dragged
us into the bankruptcy court where we got
slammed.

Chapter 21

BLEAKHOUSE

Charles Dickens wrote a novel about an estate which was litigated for years-ending when the estate had no more money to pay the attorneys. In our case, it has been nearly 10 years since Paul Hess with the help of Charles Farrington diverted the $146,000 check into their bank accounts.

Paul has since retired and purchased a one million dollar home in Seattle where he raises Alpacas.

Glenn and Charles Farrington are still in the Estate Planning business in Bellevue

On December 26th 2011, their office burned to the ground. Gone is the Cigar smoking Indian, the meerschaum pipes and oriental rugs.

Scott Easter is still practicing law at Montgomery Purdue, A proud member of the Washington Bar.

Peter Arkison awaits the next bankruptcy victim, another proud member of the Washington Bar.

Business as usual....... for Washington Lawyers.